THE
CONTAINER
GARDEN
RECIPE BOOK

THE
CONTAINER
GARDEN
RECIPE BOOK

57 Designs for Pots, Window Boxes,
Hanging Baskets, and More

LANA WILLIAMS

PHOTOGRAPHS BY ERIN SCOTT

ARTISAN | NEW YORK

To my wife, Lindsay,
for her tender heart

CONTENTS

INTRODUCTION

Magic happens when the right combination of plants and pots comes together, perfectly perched next to the front door or hanging below a window. When we spot a breathtaking container garden, it has the power to stop us in our tracks. These marvelous designs look effortless, but as you stand, paralyzed, in front of the nearly endless bounty of plants at the garden center, they can seem impossible to replicate. This book will lay out foolproof recipes for every season and teach you the guiding principles to create beautiful container gardens in a variety of sizes, shapes, and styles. These recipes are meant for everyone, whether you are planting your very first pot or are an avid gardener, and whether you're living in an urban high-rise, down a country road, or in a suburban neighborhood. The plants from each project are also listed in the Plant Index starting on page 212, with details about their growing seasons and other characteristics, which you can use as an additional reference for your own designs. Once you start your first container gardens, I promise you'll be hooked.

Many things draw us to container gardening. Maybe you are looking to increase your home's curb appeal (if so, look no further than window boxes, hanging baskets, and urns!). Maybe you long to attract birds and bees or grow your own herbs or vegetables but are dealing with limited space or poor soil. Or maybe you want to avoid weeding and the other chores that come with gardening in the ground! Whatever your motivation, creating your own container garden allows you to step away from your phone, slow down, and connect with nature.

With the world's changing and warming climate and fast-disappearing biodiversity, I believe container gardening is a political act, a radical way to help our planet. There is no need for a large yard or garden, or even a patio, to effect this change: a small pot at your front door is a beginning. Every pot planted makes a difference. Growing flowers or vegetables is a great way to reduce your carbon footprint by disrupting the demand for flowers and produce being shipped from all over the world. Container gardens can be a smart choice for conserving water, too, because you use only the amount needed to water the plants, with no excess

runoff. You can also make an impact by choosing fertilizers that will not harm the environment or animals and insects (more on this on page 20). When you give love to your containers, the plants will respond.

Like all gardens, container gardens are meant to evolve and change, and the beauty of the container garden is the ease with which this can be done. Pots can be moved and rearranged. Plants can be swapped out from spring to summer to fall. Gardening teaches us many lessons, one of which is to embrace the ebb and flow of the seasons.

I learned this lesson at an early age, at my nana's side. She owned a flower shop and maintained a lush garden, where she put me to work deadheading her pansies. I loved arriving at her house and being greeted by the ever-changing annuals in the two stone planters at her front door. When I was growing up in Arkansas, front porches were gathering places for neighbors to visit. There was an almost unspoken competition to have the best flower boxes or pots at the front door. To this day, I constantly attempt to outdo myself with each new design project, maximizing my and my clients' curb appeal.

When I moved to San Francisco for art school and into a small apartment, my personal container garden journey began. I didn't have any outdoor space, but I placed pots on my fire escape and rooftop. I had herbs, a kumquat tree, succulents, and flowers. It was a humble beginning, but the start toward creating The Tender Gardener, my Oakland-based plant business that specializes in exterior and interior plant design for businesses and private residences.

I have designed container patio gardens for bars and restaurants throughout the Bay Area, as well as balconies, front porches, private backyard oases, and interior plantscapes. My background as a painter has trained my eye: I'm always looking for unique ways to combine the colors and textures found in nature. In this book, I share things I have learned along the way. And I hope to spark your own creative genius and confidence in container gardening.

CHOOSING A CONTAINER

Essentially anything that can hold soil can be used as a container: a contemporary planter, a nineteenth-century cast-iron urn, even an old cowboy boot. The choices are endless and dictated by personal taste, budget, and style, as well as by the container's ultimate location.

First, consider the scale and type of space you want to fill and whether your container will stand alone or be part of a group. Aim for a sense of unity between your space and your containers. A traditional house, for example, is best suited to classical urns or formal planters. A new minimalist condo calls for sleek modern containers. There are places where these rules can bend, though. Perhaps you collect funky and eccentric planters that make a statement all their own, regardless of the space they are in.

Whether you're shopping for one container or many, always select the best quality you can afford. I encourage you to avoid using plastic containers: Although they are widely available and cheap—and sometimes the only solution when weight limits need to be considered, such as in window boxes—they rarely have the aesthetic appeal and visual heft of other materials. Plastic tends to fade and distort in the heat and sun and can crack

in cold weather. Some alternatives: Terra-cotta ages gracefully, becoming more patinated and full of character season after season (bring it indoors for winter in cold climates). Simple terra-cotta pots are relatively affordable and easily found secondhand. Fiberglass, often mixed with other materials like clay or stone, is a lightweight alternative manufactured in finishes that mimic any style of container. It lasts for years without fading and is virtually indestructible in all kinds of weather conditions.

Finally, ask yourself whether you want the pot to stand out or disappear. Urns, brightly colored pots, and unusually shaped and textured containers will catch the eye, and you'll need to be more mindful when selecting plants to ensure they will complement or contrast with the container. Neutral containers, like a wire hanging basket or a simple terra-cotta pot, recede into their environment and let the plants capture all the attention.

CHOOSING PLANTS

Picking out plants is my favorite part of creating a container garden. However, it's easy to get dazzled by all the amazing plants at the nursery, and you wind up coming home with a bunch of disparate plants and no plan for where to put them. The recipes that follow will guide you in choosing perfect plant combinations for dozens of eye-catching containers. Before we get to the recipes, though, here are a few overall tips:

- Always select plants that are full and healthy. Look for new growth and strong root development. A few roots dangling out of the bottom of the pot indicates a well-developed plant, just waiting for space to spread out, but a large, protruding mat of roots suggests the plant has become root-bound and will struggle to adjust in its new home; avoid those.

- When choosing flowering plants, hone in on those with lots of unopened buds rather than those with the most open flowers. This will ensure that you'll get to enjoy plenty of blooms in your garden.

- Keep an eye out for dwarf cultivars. New varieties of popular garden plants come to market every season, often propagated specifically for container

gardens. Their smaller growth habit suits container life better than those of their larger relatives, which need the root space offered in the ground.

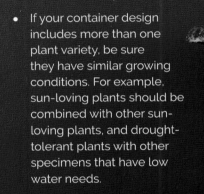

- If your container design includes more than one plant variety, be sure they have similar growing conditions. For example, sun-loving plants should be combined with other sun-loving plants, and drought-tolerant plants with other specimens that have low water needs.

MEET YOUR "INGREDIENTS"

A successful container garden design relies on combining contrasting foliage or flowers in different shapes, sizes, and growth habits in ways that make it easy to distinguish and appreciate each plant. Below are some basic "ingredient types" you can choose from. Get to know these categories and you'll be able to use the recipes that follow as a guide, mixing and matching different varieties that speak to you within each category.

INGREDIENT ROLES

THRILLERS
Plants that are the focal point of an arrangement, often with showy blooms or dramatic foliage. Examples include Sallyfun 'Bicolor Blue' salvia (*Salvia farinacea*; pictured), 'Camelot Lavender' foxglove (*Digitalis purpurea*), and 'Crinoline Ruffles' echeveria (*Echeveria*).

SPILLERS
Plants with foliage or flowers that grow downward and trail out the sides of containers. Examples include Scopia 'Gulliver Blue' bacopa (*Chaenostoma cordatum*; pictured), 'Goldilocks' creeping Jennys (*Lysimachia nummularia*), and fishhooks (*Senecio radicans*).

FILLERS
Plants that add texture and fill the gaps between taller and trailing plants. Examples include asparagus fern (*Asparagus densiflorus*; pictured), grasses, and ground covers like blue fescue (*Festuca idahoensis*) and silver carpet (*Dymondia margaretae*).

ARCHITECTURAL PLANTS
Plants with strong lines and interesting forms that stand out and utilize negative space in a design. Examples include kangaroo paw (*Anigozanthos flavidus*; pictured), cat tails euphorbia (*Euphorbia leucadendron*), and century plant (*Agave americana*).

INGREDIENT PALETTES

Color is another key element in a successful design. Whether you choose a monochromatic planting or a high-contrast color combination, you'll find many plant varieties within each color palette category listed below. And be aware that these colors come in a range of ingredient roles. In other words, you can find a lemon-lime filler as well as a lemon-lime spiller, so consider which role *and* color would function best in combination with the other plants in the container.

DARK FOLIAGE

These dramatic beauties add depth and contrast thanks to their deep purple leaves. They pair well with pale flowers or silver or lemon-lime foliage. Examples include 'Illusion Midnight Lace' sweet potato vine (*Ipomoea batatas*; pictured), 'Nigrescens' black mondo grass (*Ophiopogon planiscapus*), and 'Dark Opal' purple basil (*Ocimum basilicum*).

SILVER, BLUE, AND GRAY FOLIAGE

These cool colors can illuminate a shady corner or provide a light touch in the summer sun. They contrast well with dark foliage and complement blue, purple, burgundy, orange, and pale flowers. Examples include bush morning glory (*Convolvulus cneorum*; pictured), dusty miller (*Jacobaea maritima*), and 'Blue Pearl' sedum (*Hylotelephium*).

LEMON-LIME FOLIAGE

Use plants with almost-electric foliage to brighten up shady spots or jazz up a container. These pair well with dark foliage and flowers in pinks, purples, oranges, reds, and yellows. Examples include 'Limewire' coleus (*Plectranthus scutellarioides*; pictured), Scotch moss (*Arenaria verna 'Aurea'*), and 'Lime Marmalade' coralbells (*Heuchera*).

COLORFUL FOLIAGE

In garden design, green is the default neutral. By introducing colorful foliage, you add lasting color to a container, with or without flowers. Look for options with bicolor or multicolored foliage. Examples include 'Carolyn Wharton' caladium (*Caladium hortulanum*; pictured) and multicolored coleus (*Plectranthus scutellarioides*).

TOOLS

Having sharp, clean, and organized tools makes gardening more enjoyable. When you're excited to pot up your new plants and reach for your spade, you want to know exactly where it is and that it's ready to be used. These are the tools you'll need to start and maintain your container gardens.

1. SMALL SCISSORS. Perfect for snipping the tiniest of flowers and stems.

2. GARDEN SNIPS (IDEALLY SPRING-LOADED). My number one tool for easy and precise pruning and deadheading (removing flowers that have finished blooming).

3. HAND PRUNING SHEARS. Best for pruning woody stems.

4. LEATHER GLOVES. To keep your hands clean and protected from skin-irritating sap or spiky cacti.

5. SPADE. For scooping soil and dislodging stuck plants from the sides of a container.

6. HAND FORK. For breaking up dense soil, mixing soil, and unpotting stuck plants by loosening the root-ball.

7. LARGE WATERING CAN. To minimize trips to the spigot. Purchase one with a long spout, which makes it easy to reach the base of a plant. If you can, select a watering can with a detachable rosette. The rosette releases water slowly (ideal for delicate plants and seedlings) and has a wider radius, making it easier to reach the entire surface of the pot. Remove the rosette and the spout provides a faster and more precise flow of water, although you'll have to be more intentional to ensure all roots get a drink.

SOIL

The recipes in this book feature two types of soil: an all-purpose potting mix and a succulent and cactus potting mix. As tempting as it might be to use soil from the earth when potting your plants, it's best to avoid this. Ground soil may contain pathogens (diseases), insect pests, and weeds, and it is denser and thus compacts in containers, resulting in stunted plants.

Most all-purpose potting mixes on the market contain some blend of sphagnum peat moss or coco coir (coconut fiber) to retain moisture; compost to provide nutrients; and perlite, vermiculite, sand, and bark to aerate the soil and improve drainage. Peat moss does its job well, but it is not a renewable resource. It is taken from bogs that are thousands of years old at a rate that is unsustainable.

Coco coir is a common alternative because it is lightweight and excellent at retaining moisture. Made from the pith (the fiber between the husks and shells) of coconuts and once considered a waste product of the coconut industry, coco coir is an abundant raw material yet not without controversy. Significant manual labor and water are required to process the pith into coco coir, among other concerns. Soil scientists and researchers are working toward developing more sustainable and regenerative alternatives to peat moss and coco coir–based potting mixes. Hopefully, we will see these products available soon.

Because succulents and cacti are drought tolerant and sensitive to overwatering, they require a special potting mix, one that omits moisture-retaining elements like coco coir or peat moss and instead includes sand and grit for drainage. Always use a succulent and cactus mix when potting these plants.

POTTING 101

CLEANING

If you are using a pot that previously had something planted in it, wash it out with water and scrub until clean using a firm bristled brush. If the container's previous plants had any sort of pest or disease, wash the pot, then sterilize it with diluted bleach water (one part bleach to nine parts water). This will prevent any contamination of the newly potted plants. (*Note:* Always dispose of diseased plant material and soil in the trash and not in your compost pile or the city compost.)

DRAINAGE

All plants need drainage. Without drain holes, water cannot escape, and plant roots will be susceptible to root rot, which will eventually kill the plant. If you have a container with no drainage, you can either use it as a cachepot (a decorative pot that holds a smaller, draining pot and saucer) or drill holes in the container. Your local hardware store will carry drill bits for ceramic, concrete, metal, and plastic; use the correct type to prevent the pot from breaking.

CROCKS AND ROCKS

When using a large container, you may wish to place a few curved crocks or rocks over the drain hole before filling the pot with soil, to prevent the weight of the plants and soil from plugging the drain hole. In small and medium-size containers, it's not necessary to add crocks or rocks over the drain hole, although it won't hurt to do so. Alternatively, in smaller pots, cover the drain hole with a piece of mesh so water passes through but soil can't escape.

    Note: Never place a whole layer of rocks on the bottom of a container. This can eventually cause root damage, because the roots will grow around the rocks, making it difficult to repot later without damaging both the roots and the pot.

HOW TO POT

1. Set up in a place you don't mind getting dirty. Select your container. If it's a used container, rinse out any old soil. For larger pots, place a few rocks or crocks in the bottom of the container to cover the drain hole.

2. Add soil until the crown of the largest potted plant's root-ball sits an inch or two (2.5 to 5 cm) below the container rim. Be careful not to cover or bury plant stems above the root-ball, as this can cause stem rot. (There are some exceptions to this rule—for example, when planting tomatoes, you often bury a good portion of the stem. Roots will form along the stem, which will help anchor and bring more water and nutrients to the plant.)

3. Starting with your largest plant, remove it from its nursery pot and examine the roots. If the plant is root-bound, meaning the roots are densely packed or are wrapping round and round the bottom of the pot, gently massage the roots to loosen them. In extreme cases, use clean scissors to cut an X across the bottom of the plant to break roots free. Cutting the roots stimulates new growth and encourages the roots to spread out in their new home. If the plant is not root-bound, simply pop it out of its nursery pot and plant it directly into the container soil. (Plants with fine hairlike roots, such as hellebores and poppies, are very sensitive to root disturbance, so it's best to leave their roots alone.)

4. If you are planting smaller plants in the same container with larger plants, add more soil to the container so that the top of each root-ball will sit at the same height as that of the larger plants.

Once you've placed all your plants, fill the gaps with soil. Using your fingers, push the soil into the holes so that it is firmly packed. Top off with more soil, if needed. Now water in the plants. Don't skip this step! Watering immediately after planting helps the soil settle, hydrates the plants, prevents air gaps around the roots that could cause the plants to dry out, and encourages the roots to spread in their new pot.

CARING FOR YOUR PLANTS

WATERING

Container gardens require a watchful eye regarding their watering needs. Because the plant roots can't grow deep into the earth to seek out water, we are responsible for providing them the moisture they need (except, of course, when it rains!). Containers are raised off the ground and thus more exposed to the elements, which makes their soil dry out faster than ground soil. Additionally, porous containers like terra-cotta and moss-lined hanging baskets dry out more quickly than glazed ceramic, fiberglass, or plastic.

Containers also dry out at different rates depending on outdoor temperatures, pot size, and location. In winter and during rainy periods, containers dry out more slowly than they do in summer or hot weather. Pots in the shade retain moisture longer than pots in the sun.

Check each container before watering to gauge its moisture level. This can be done in several ways: For plants that need frequent watering but can't tolerate soggy conditions, stick your finger at least two knuckles deep into the soil. If you feel moisture, wait another day and check again. Looking at leaves and flowers is another way to tell when plants need moisture. Drooping and browning leaves, as well as prematurely drying or wilting flowers, are signs of underwatering; yellowing foliage usually indicates overwatering. That said, overwatered plants may also display drooping leaves, so be sure to check the soil before turning on the spigot. For very large containers, a moisture meter can be helpful: these have long metal probes that you stick deep into the soil, and the meter indicates whether the soil is wet or dry.

Here are more best practices for watering:

- Water the entire root-ball, not just one section of a container.

- Always water at the soil level, not on the leaves. Plants absorb water through their roots. Water that sits on leaves can act like a magnifying glass, and direct sunlight passing through the water droplets can burn the wet leaves.

- Water deeply: that is, until you see water running out the drain holes.

- Water early in the morning or in the evening. Water applied in the heat of the day can evaporate before the roots have a chance to soak it up, and can burn the leaves. Morning watering is preferred, as nighttime watering can lead to fungal disease issues.

Each recipe in this book has a watering guide. This is what each term means:

HIGH: Plants need water multiple times a week. During heat waves or hot weather, check containers daily.

MODERATE: Plants need watering at least once a week.

LOW: Plants need watering every one to two weeks or when the soil is almost dry. (Cacti like to dry out completely between watering.)

FERTILIZER

Plants need more than just water—they also require nutrients. A plant that grows in the ground pulls nutrients from the soil, requiring less-frequent fertilizing. But plants in containers have access only to the limited nutrients in the potting mix, which can quickly be used up and leach out of the container every time it is watered. Regularly fertilizing is therefore necessary to provide container plants with the nutrients they need to thrive.

Plants need the most nutrients from spring through fall, when most plants are actively growing. Best practice is to add a slow-release fertilizer according to the manufacturer's instructions when you pot your plants, and supplement it with a water-soluble liquid fertilizer every six weeks from spring to fall. In winter, you can typically stop fertilizing, as most plants go dormant. For the exceptions—winter-flowering plants like cyclamens or pansies—you continue to fertilize as long as they are in bloom. Always water your plants before fertilizing them, which will prevent fertilizer burn (discoloration or root damage caused by the salts in the fertilizer drawing out too much moisture).

I encourage you to choose a natural or organic fertilizer over a synthetic (petroleum-based) product. Because synthetic fertilizers are more concentrated, it's too easy to overfertilize, which can kill or damage plants and run off and pollute groundwater. Natural fertilizers are gentler and leave less salt buildup in containers. Alfalfa meal, fish pellets, bat guano, and worm castings are my favorite slow-release fertilizers. When it comes to liquid fertilizers, my go-tos are an all-purpose complete and balanced fertilizer or fish and kelp fertilizer. Follow the recommended dosage.

Look for fertilizers that contain a mixture of micro- and macronutrients, which are super beneficial to your plants. When shopping for fertilizers, you may notice three numbers. Those numbers are the percentage of nitrogen, phosphorus, and potassium—three macronutrients that all plants need. Nitrogen (N) produces leafy growth. Phosphorus (P) promotes strong root growth and encourages flowers and fruit. Potassium (K) promotes vigorous growth and hardiness. A complete fertilizer will contain all three, and a balanced fertilizer will have equal amounts of N, P, and K. Note that higher NPK numbers on fertilizers aren't necessarily better. Natural organic fertilizers have lower numbers because they release their nutrients slowly over a longer period of time. Be aware that there are fertilizers tailored for specific plants, but specialty products generally aren't necessary. As long as you apply an organic, balanced fertilizer, your plants will get the nutrients they need.

Note: The exact wrong time to start fertilizing is when your plants are in decline. Rather, you want to fertilize when a plant is healthy and pushing out new growth. (See page 22 for more on what to do if you notice your plants are looking poorly.)

LIGHT

Light is the most important consideration when choosing plants for a space. All plants require light, even those that grow in shade. Understanding the quality of light in a space can be difficult, as it changes throughout the seasons. When designing for a container garden, it's best to select plants based on the light they will receive in summer (when they are actively growing) rather than winter. If light conditions in a certain spot vary widely from summer to winter, you may want to move the plant—luckily, most containers are pretty portable! Avoid mixing sun-loving and shade-loving plants in the same container, otherwise one or the other won't be happy. And keep in mind that morning sun is less intense than afternoon sun, so many plants that prefer shade can tolerate some morning direct sun.

Each recipe in this book specifies the plants' light preferences, using these standard definitions (which will also help you decode labels when picking out plants at nurseries):

FULL SUN: Receives six or more hours of direct sunlight a day.

PARTIAL SUN: Receives four to six hours of direct sunlight a day, favoring afternoon sun.

PARTIAL SHADE: Receives four to six hours of direct sunlight a day, favoring afternoon shade.

SHADE: Receives fewer than four hours of direct sunlight a day, without afternoon sun, or no direct sun.

PLANT SOS

If a plant is looking sad and bedraggled, consider these factors:

CONDITIONS. First, are you meeting the plant's needs? Does it have the proper water, soil, and light conditions? If not, it won't thrive. For more on this, see pages 16–21.

LIFE CYCLE. Is the plant an annual? If so, it may have run its course. Changing seasons can affect appearance as well: some flowering plants bloom for only one season; others bloom for multiple seasons. Weather changes also trigger deciduous plants to drop their leaves, which is a normal part of the plants' life cycle. Many perennials die back all the way to the ground when they enter their dormant period, but their roots are full of life, and new growth will emerge when conditions are right. (If you don't want to live with a bare spot in your container when a plant goes dormant, you can find it a new home in the garden, compost it, or plant something bushy next to it that will hide the bare spot.)

INSECT INFESTATION. Check plants often, even when they appear healthy, to catch any pest problems early. Insects often hide on the undersides of leaves and seek out tender new growth. Look for holes in leaves, curling, unusual spots, and yellowing or other leaf discoloration. For help identifying specific pests, check out the Resources on page 210.

If you find aphids, whiteflies, thrips, or other visible pests, your first step is to apply a strong stream of water with a garden hose to knock them off the plants. Then look for ways to deter the pest. The least invasive approach is to introduce a companion plant that naturally repels the insect. For example, marigolds, catnip, peppermint, chives, and other plants with strong fragrances keep aphids away. Place one of these next to the infected plant or tuck a few into the same pot. (Your local nursery can

provide companion planting suggestions, or see the Resources on page 211.)

The next step would be to encourage predatory insects such as green lacewings, ladybugs, hoverflies, and parasitic wasps. These critters, also known as beneficial insects, eat many different soft-bodied pests. There are specific plants these predatory insects love that will lure them to your garden. Alternatively, you can purchase predatory insects at your local specialty nursery or online. Just be sure to grow a variety of plants that will encourage these insects to stay in your garden.

If plants and predatory insects fail to control the pests, the next line of defense is a natural insecticide, such as neem oil. Derived from the neem plant, neem oil works against soft-bodied insects as well as fungal diseases like powdery mildew and black spot (more on these on the next page). For neem oil to be effective, it must come into contact with the pest you

Aphids

are trying to remove. Be sure no beneficial insects are on the plant you're treating. Spray all sides of the plant's leaves in the early morning or the evening, when beneficial insects are less active. Avoid spraying plants in the heat of the day because neem oil can cause leaf burn in direct sun. Neem oil works against pests only when it is wet, and it takes about an hour to dry, so you may need to reapply the oil every few days to remove the pests.

SLUGS AND SNAILS. If you find holes in the middle of leaves or chewed-up leaf edges, chances are you are dealing with slugs or snails. One trick that prevents these mollusks from climbing into containers is to wrap copper tape around the base of a pot or near the rim. A chemical reaction occurs when they come in contact with copper, deterring them from crossing the tape but leaving the slugs and snails unharmed. Just be sure to leave no gaps where they could cross. I prefer the tape over snail and slug pellets, which birds and wildlife easily mistake for food and can cause them harm. Other natural deterrents are crushed-up eggshells, as mollusks don't like to cross the jagged edges. Nor do slugs and snails like the bitter taste of coffee grounds, which can be sprinkled around the base of plants.

DISEASE. Plant diseases are often named by the appearance of the damage they cause to plants, such as black spot, rust, and powdery mildew. These are quite common, but there are easy steps to help prevent them. First and foremost, regularly look at your plants. If you notice any abnormal development, immediately remove the affected leaves. Second, keep the soil around the plants clean by picking up dead or fallen plant debris. Finally, most of these diseases grow in moist and humid environments, so try to water the base of the plants, rather than the leaves.

For more in-depth information on how to treat specific plants for specific pests and diseases, check out the Resources on page 210.

Snail

Black spot

PLANT MAINTENANCE

DEADHEADING

Deadheading is the best way to keep your container full of flowers. Deadheading means pinching or snipping off dead or dying flowers to prevent them from going to seed; this encourages the plant to produce more blooms. You can deadhead by pinching with your thumbnail and index finger or by using snips to cut where the flower stalk meets the stem of the plant. Avoid popping off the head of the flower only, leaving a sad, bare stalk.

PRUNING

Pruning is the act of selectively removing parts of a plant to improve its health or control its growth. Always use sharp and clean tools when pruning, and clean your tools with rubbing alcohol when moving between plants to help prevent the spread of disease. For tender plants, snips will do the job, but for woodier branches, shears will provide a cleaner cut. For thick tree branches, you will need to bring out the loppers. Pruning is often done in late fall or winter to encourage new spring growth. There are some exceptions, though: Early bloomers, such as azaleas, big-leaf hydrangeas, and lilacs, set buds in winter, so you'll want to wait to prune these until after the plants have flowered. Summer pruning is often done on fruiting and ornamental trees to redirect and concentrate the plants' energy on fruiting buds.

Pruning plants encourages full, healthy growth. You may choose to prune if you notice growth that has become leggy or thin. Cut back to just above the leaf nodes or small leaf buds to encourage side shoots. (Leaf nodes are the points on a stem where there are small bumps or swelling where new stems or leaves will emerge.) You'll also want to prune damaged stems or branches to preserve the health of the plant.

REFRESHING POTTED PLANTS

After a plant has been in a container for some time, you may notice it has sunk in its pot. Or you may see lots of perlite (the white particles in potting mix) on the surface of the soil and soil that looks gray. These are signs the plant has used up the soil nutrients.

To remedy a sunken plant, unpot it, shake off any loose soil from the roots, and place fresh potting soil in the bottom of the container before returning the plant to its home. Fill in any gaps with new soil and then water the container.

(*Note:* Sometimes it can be difficult to remove plants from pots they have grown in for a long time. Here's a proven method: First, take a spade or shovel and work your way around the edge of the pot to loosen any roots stuck to the container. Gently tip the pot on its side and use the spade to scooch out the root-ball.)

If the plant hasn't sunk but the soil looks depleted, replenish its nutrients by topping off the pot with fresh potting mix. This method is particularly useful for large, cumbersome containers and plants that may be too difficult to completely repot. First, scrape back the top 3 to 4 inches (7.6 to 10 cm) of soil. Be gentle if you come to a mass of roots—try not to rip them out. Your goal is to end up with a trench around your plants and some exposed roots. Using fresh soil, fill in the holes and water in the soil.

Root pruning is also beneficial for the health of plants that have lived in the same container for a long time and have become root-bound, as well as for vigorous growers that have outgrown their pot but that you want to keep in the same container. To root prune, first remove the plant from the container. With clean shears or a knife, remove up to one-third of the plant's roots and loosen compacted soil. Fill the container with fresh potting mix and repot the plant at the desired height. Water in the plant.

WINTERIZING YOUR CONTAINER GARDEN

In climates that dip below freezing, many plants and pots will need to be protected from harsh winter weather. While all plants have different hardiness, if you live in USDA Hardiness Zone 8 or below, keeping some plants alive in containers over winter is a real challenge (for more on climate zones, see box below). If you live in a chilly zone, or where temperatures are often below freezing during winter, you may opt to start fresh with new plants each spring. If you wish to keep your planters year-round, the safest bet is to bring them inside or into a greenhouse, garage, or shed where they will still receive light but will be protected from freezing.

The foliage of winter-hardy plants is adapted to surviving year-round, but the roots of these plants are used to being warm and protected in the earth; when they are aboveground, they are less hardy than their listed zone suggests. If leaving plants in containers over winter, choose plants at least two zones above your actual planting zone.

Pots themselves are also susceptible to winter weather damage. Water expands when it freezes, which can wreck containers. Porous containers, like terra-cotta, are easily damaged in winter, so it's best to clean and store the pots upside down or on their side in a dry place. Over time, even flexible materials like plastic can crack. Fiberglass pots are one of the best materials for freezing weather. Wood is also flexible and durable.

If you must leave plants outside, you can take several steps to help protect them:

- In places where there are only occasional freezing temperatures, move pots to shelter and cover with blankets when there is a threat of frost.

- Elevate pots on bricks or risers specifically made for planters so water can freely drain. If possible, set containers on earth instead of pavement, which can quickly heat up and cool down throughout the day, stressing roots.

- Remove any saucers that will hold water underneath your pots, as this water will freeze.

- Wrap containers in blankets, bubble wrap, or burlap to provide extra insulation. You can also stick your pot in a bag and fill it with straw.

- Dig a hole in your garden and bury the pot for the winter with the plants inside it.

- Group pots together, with the hardiest plants on the outside and straw between the pots for insulation.

- Place containers next to a wall or fence to help shield plants from cold winds.

When the weather begins to warm and new growth appears, it is safe to remove the winter protection.

KNOW YOUR CLIMATE ZONE

The USDA Plant Hardiness Zone Map is an important tool for US gardeners and growers to determine which plants are most likely to thrive in their locations. The map, which is divided into 13 zones (plus subzones) based on the average annual minimum winter temperature, can be found at planthardiness.ars.usda.gov.

SPECIAL TECHNIQUES

PLANTING BULBS

Growing flowers from bulbs in containers is extremely satisfying, particularly when you see the first bits of green peeking through the soil. If you live in a colder, frost-prone climate, plant bulbs in fall before the ground gets too hard or freezes; in mild climates that never or rarely get frost, you can plant bulbs as late as early winter.

Tulips and other spring bulbs have to be tricked into winter dormancy in mild climates by being chilled for twelve weeks or so in a refrigerator before they are planted. (I have a special mini-fridge just for bulbs, because ethylene gas, given off by some foods, like apples and onions, can sterilize bulbs.) If you skip chilling your bulbs, your flowers will bloom at ground level, without any stem. Some local nurseries sell prechilled bulbs.

As a general rule, plant bulbs and corms at a depth two to three times their size.

1. Fill your container two-thirds of the way with potting mix.

2. Add a layer of bulbs close together, pointy sides up, so that they are almost touching.

3. Cover with a layer of soil.

4. Add another layer of bulbs.

5. Cover with another layer of soil. Depending on the size and depth of the pot, you can repeat steps 3 and 4 several times. In a 12-inch (30.5 cm) pot, you should be able to fit twenty bulbs for a very full look.

6. Top off the pot with soil. You can also place a layer of decorative rocks on the soil. This both looks nice and deters hungry critters from digging up your bulbs. In colder climates, be sure to protect your pots from cracking in deep freezes (see the winterizing tips on page 25).

LINING A HANGING BASKET WITH LIVING MOSS

Living moss, like the Irish moss shown here, makes a lush green liner for wire hanging baskets and is a fun alternative to the more commonly seen preserved moss or coco coir liners. You'll need about thirty 2-inch (5 cm) moss plants to cover a 12-inch (30.5 cm) hanging basket.

Notes: You'll want to buy 2-inch (5 cm) plants because they have shallow enough roots to leave room for other plants inside the container. Choose a basket with small gaps between the wires to help prevent the moss from falling through the cracks.

1. Set the hanging basket on top of an empty container to stabilize the basket while planting it. Start at the bottom center of the basket and arrange the moss so the roots are facing the interior of the container. Moss plants often come in little rectangular shapes; place the individual plants horizontally with the metal vertical wires in the center of an individual plant so it doesn't fall through the holes.

2. Work your way around the base of the basket, fitting the plants snugly together.

A living moss liner requires a little extra attention when watering the hanging basket, as you'll need to ensure you are watering all parts of the soil and giving the moss a drink, too. I like to use a hose because it's easier to soak the entire basket and spray the moss from all directions.

3. Continue to plant the moss plants adjacent to one another, layer by layer, until you reach the rim of the basket.

4. When you complete the moss lining, you will be left with a hole in the center to plant in.

DESIGN PRINCIPLES

DESIGNING A CONTAINER

- A successful container design features plants of different heights, textures, and growth habits. You want tall varieties to plant at the back of the container and low-growing or spiller plants trailing over the edge toward the front of containers. For more on plant types, see pages 12–13.

- Consider the negative space created by the plants' foliage—the gaps between the leaves are as important as the showstopper flower. A successful composition isn't always the most packed planter.

- Always give your plant a 360-degree look before planting it to decide the best angle and direction to place it in the container. Most often flowers and foliage should spill outward beyond the edge of the container to create a full look.

ARRANGING POTS

- When grouping multiple pots together, keep in mind how the plants will combine with neighboring plants in the nearby containers. For example, you might want one pot filled with all low-growing or trailing plants because of its role and function within a larger group of containers. Within groups of containers, using repetition in either plant, color, or texture helps create unity.

- Place taller pots in the back and smaller pots in the front to allow all the plants to be seen and create more visual interest in your grouping. If you don't have a tall pot, elevate shorter pots by stacking them on top of upside-down planters; the smaller pots you place in front will hide your trick.

- Having too-small containers for a space is one of the most common design mistakes. Even in small spaces, a few large containers with large plants will have a greater visual impact than many small pots.

- The triangle is a compositional device often used by artists to draw the viewer's eye to a focal point. Use this same principle when designing your container garden to create successful "compositions." A grouping of three pots is the simplest way to play with this design principle, but the same idea can be used with larger groupings, too. And the tallest pot doesn't have to be the apex of the triangle: get creative by using a low-growing trailing plant in the tallest pot and a short pot with a tall plant as the apex.

1

POTS

The most versatile and widely accessible containers, pots are available in an infinite variety of shapes, sizes, and materials—and the possibilities for planting are just as vast. The recipes in this chapter represent a range of aesthetic styles, from contemporary to traditional options, and container plantings suitable for both sunny settings and shady spots. In some recipes, we'll choose plants to show off details of a special container, while in other arrangements, the plants are the star. Either way, this chapter will teach you how to play off the shapes, textures, and colors of your chosen pots when making plant selections.

EGYPTIAN TERRA-COTTA

SEASONS: Spring through fall
LIGHT: Partial shade to shade
WATER: High

PLANTS

One 1-gallon (4 L) Northern Exposure Amber coralbells (*Heuchera* 'TNHEUNEA')

One 6-inch (15 cm) angel wing begonia (*Begonia × argenteo guttata*)

One 4-inch (10 cm) rosy maidenhair fern (*Adiantum hispidulum*)

CONTAINER & MATERIALS

12-inch-diameter (30 cm) terra-cotta planter

Potting mix

In this moody arrangement, dramatic foliage is the star. Rather than showy flowers, the intricacies of each plant's leaves draw us in. The uncommon amber foliage of coralbells and the maidenhair fern's coppery new growth bring out the warmth of the terra-cotta pot. The plants' upright and mounding growth habits show off the key decorative features of the planter: its hourglass shape and piecrust rim.

1. Fill the pot three-quarters of the way with potting mix. Place the largest plant, the coralbells, on the left side of the pot. It should sit an inch or two (2.5 to 5 cm) below the rim; add or remove soil as needed to reach this height. Then pack a few handfuls of soil around the root-ball to hold it in place.

2. Next, place the begonia toward the back of the pot, at the same height as the coralbells (add or remove soil as needed to ensure it's not too deep or too shallow). This type of begonia has an upright growth habit and can get quite tall, so it is best placed at the back of the arrangement. If it ever gets too tall for its own weight, use bamboo stakes to help it stand upright.

3. Add more soil to the container so that the fern will sit level with the other plants, then place the fern in the front right space. Fill the gaps with soil and water in the plants.

TERRA-COTTA TRIO

'Cambridge Blue' lobelia

'Tête-à-Tête' narcissus

Durango Orange French marigold

'Cheerfulness'
double narcissus

orange star

variegated
nasturtium

TERRA-COTTA TRIO

SEASON: Spring
LIGHT: Full sun
WATER: High

PLANTS

Four 2-inch (5 cm) Durango Orange French marigolds (*Tagetes patula* 'PAS97727')

One 6-inch (15 cm) 'Tête-à-Tête' narcissus (*Narcissus*)

Four 4-inch (10 cm) 'Cambridge Blue' lobelias (*Lobelia erinus*)

One 6-inch (15 cm) 'Cheerfulness' double narcissus (*Narcissus*)

One cell pack of six 2-inch (5 cm) variegated nasturtiums (*Tropaeolum majus*)

Two 3-inch (5 cm) orange stars (*Ornithogalum dubium*)

CONTAINERS & MATERIALS

Potting mix

One 6-inch-diameter (15 cm) terra-cotta planter

One 13-inch-diameter (33 cm) shallow terra-cotta bowl

One 10-inch-diameter (25 cm) terra-cotta planter

This sun-loving arrangement celebrates spring with full pots bursting with color. When designing with multiple pots, repetition of color, texture, or plants helps keep the grouping cohesive. Here all three pots are made of the same material, and at least one shared plant element in each pot ties the arrangement together. Though all three pots are terra-cotta, choosing vessels with different heights and shapes creates visual interest and ensures all the plants can be seen. (The head pot was a special find made by Ruth Easterbrook.)

1. Place potting mix in the bottom of the smallest pot so that the plants will sit just below the rim. Squeeze four marigolds into the pot and fill the gaps between the root-balls with soil.

2. Place soil in the bottom of the shallow bowl. Set the 'Tête-à-Tête' narcissus in the center to sit an inch (2.5 cm) below the rim; add or remove soil as needed to reach this height. Evenly space the four lobelias around the edge of the pot. All the plants should sit at the same height. Fill in all the gaps with soil.

3. Fill the tallest pot halfway with soil. Place the double narcissus in the center of the pot to sit just below the rim. Add more soil to hold the plant in place, and raise the soil level for the smaller plants. Evenly space the six nasturtiums around the pot rim. Fit the two orange star plants between the nasturtiums and narcissus, one toward the front of the container and one toward the back. Fill the gaps with soil.

4. Water in the plants in all three containers.

Daffodil, Jonquil, and Narcissus

PLANT TYPE: Perennial bulb

SEASON: Spring

LIGHT: Partial shade to full sun, depending on variety

WATER: Moderate

AVAILABLE COLORS: White, cream, orange, coral, yellow, bicolor

Nothing heralds the arrival of spring like plants in the *Narcissus* genus. These are among the first flowers to greet the cool, crisp air and signal the end of winter. Frequently called by their common names—daffodils, jonquils, or narcissus—these blossoms can be recognized by the distinctive corona or trumpet shape that protrudes from their petals, which is part of the flower structure that surrounds the stamen. Though you may be most familiar with the bright yellow varieties, these spring beauties come in a range of color combinations, as well as different shapes, sizes, and scents. Some have a single row of petals, while others (called doubles) have two or more rows of petals, giving them a frilly appearance.

You can never go wrong adding a pot of daffodils to your space for spring. Whether you place it by your door, set it on a table, or group it with other containers, growing *Narcissus* in a pot is a great way to take advantage of its wonderful intoxicating scent (their fragrance is what makes them one of my favorite bulbs). And the more the merrier! Don't be afraid to layer and pack them close together in the container if growing from bulbs (see page 26 for more on this).

Nasturtium

Nasturtiums (from the genus *Tropaeolum*) are one of the easiest and fastest-growing plants you can add to your outdoor space. These cool-weather-loving plants look equally beautiful climbing up a trellis or trailing down a pot or basket. Excellent fillers and spillers, they provide lush foliage with cute round green or variegated leaves and colorful tubular flowers in all shades of red, orange, and yellow. To encourage abundant blooms, place them in full sun, although they tolerate partial shade.

You've probably seen nasturtium flowers in a salad, but every part of the plant is edible and has a refreshing, peppery taste. Snip a few leaves off to try with your next meal (or cut some flowers to display in a vase)—the plant will quickly send out more new growth and is undeterred by pruning. The blossoms are wonderful for attracting pollinators, and after the flowers wilt on the vine, you'll end up with seeds (also edible). If you have a flower bed nearby, you'll likely see some volunteers pop up. ("Volunteer" plants are those that you do not plant but grow on their own.) When there are at least two different-colored varieties, cross-pollination will deliver interesting new shades of colors on plants the following year!

PLANT TYPE: Annual

SEASONS: Spring, early summer, fall

LIGHT: Full sun to partial shade

WATER: Moderate

AVAILABLE COLORS: Red, orange, yellow, bicolor

PAINTED TERRA-COTTA

SEASONS: Spring through fall
LIGHT: Full sun to partial shade
WATER: Moderate

PLANTS

One 5-gallon (19 L) 'Tamukeyama' lacy Japanese maple (*Acer palmatum* var. *dissectum*)

One 1-gallon (4 L) Australian astroturf (*Scleranthus biflorus*)

Two 4-inch (10 cm) Australian astroturfs (*Scleranthus biflorus*)

Three 4-inch (10 cm) 'Nigrescens' black mondo grass (*Ophiopogon planiscapus*)

Sixteen 2-inch (5 cm) baby's tears (*Soleirolia soleirolii*)

CONTAINER & MATERIALS

A few curved crocks or rocks

24-inch-diameter (61 cm) painted terra-cotta planter

Potting mix

Three lava rocks

Small or dwarf trees can make a big impact in container gardens. They can stand alone as a focal point, or a pair can be used to flank a door or divide a space. When planting trees in containers, take advantage of the opportunity for underplanting (planting smaller plants below larger plants and trees), which helps naturalize the tree and adds visual interest where there would otherwise be bare soil. Underplanting with winter-hardy plants also keeps a container interesting during winter if the tree is deciduous (meaning it drops its leaves in winter), like the Japanese maple used here. When underplanting, be sure your pot is large enough to accommodate the additional plants, and choose shallow-rooted plants that will not compete with the tree, such as low-growing plants (like violas, cyclamen, and petunias) and those used for ground cover (Scotch or Irish moss, dymondia, and mondo grass).

1. Place the crocks or rocks over the drainage hole of the planter to help prevent soil compaction (see pages 17–18 for more on this). Add a layer of potting mix so that when you place your tree in the container the trunk sits an inch or two (2.5 to 5 cm) below the rim. Insert the tree, then gently knock loose the top layer of soil so that you can nestle plants on top in the following steps.

2. Add soil around the tree so that the next largest plant, the 1-gallon (4 L) astroturf, sits at the same depth. Place the astroturf toward the front right side of the container.

3. Add more soil so that the two 4-inch (10 cm) astroturfs sit at an even depth with the other plants and place at the front and left side of the container. Add the black mondo grass plants, one toward the back left, one to the right of the tree trunk, and the third on the right edge of the container.

4. Next, arrange the lava rocks. I placed two near the base of the tree (to fill the gap where it was harder to plant over its roots) and one on its own, so that the arrangement would feel more natural.

5. Add more soil so that the baby's tears sit at the same depth as the other plants. Plant these to fill in all the gaps in the plantings, creating the mossy finish to the miniature forest floor. Water in the plants.

SEASONS: Spring through fall
LIGHT: Full to partial sun
WATER: Moderate

PLANTS

One 1-gallon (4 L) ti plant
(*Cordyline fruticosa*)

Two 4-inch (10 cm) 'Lime Marmalade'
coralbells (*Heuchera*)

Six 2-inch (5 cm) Sorbet XP Yellow
violas (*Viola cornuta* 'PAS1241263')

Five 3-inch (8 cm) multicolored coleus
(*Plectranthus scutellarioides*)

CONTAINER & MATERIALS

12-inch-diameter (30 cm) peach
glazed ceramic planter

Potting mix

1 Fill the pot three-quarters of the way with potting mix. Place the ti plant at the back right edge of the container, to establish the asymmetrical composition.

2 Add more soil, until it is 5 inches (13 cm) from the rim. Place the two coralbells in the center of the pot. Fill in more soil around the plants so that the remaining plants will sit at the same height.

3 Alternate the violas and coleus around the perimeter of the pot. Fill the gaps with soil and water in the plants.

VINTAGE TERRA-COTTA

SEASONS: All
LIGHT: Full to partial sun
WATER: Low

PLANTS

One 1-gallon (4 L) 'Rubra' African milk tree (*Euphorbia trigona*)

One 24-inch (61 cm) flat of 'Murale' white stonecrop (*Sedum album* subsp. *teretifolium*)

CONTAINER & MATERIALS

A few curved crocks or rocks

20-inch-diameter (51 cm) terra-cotta planter with handles

Succulent and cactus potting mix

This is a simple pairing with a dramatic impact. The African milk tree is a striking plant that looks like a cactus but is in fact a succulent. It is underplanted with a low-growing stonecrop that gracefully spills over the lip of the planter. Its low profile accentuates the height of the African milk tree, and it makes a happy companion plant because they share the same light and water needs. In mild climates this arrangement will thrive outside year-round. If you live where temperatures dip below freezing, bring it inside to overwinter in a sunny window.

1. Place the crocks or rocks over the drain hole of the planter. Fill the container three-quarters of the way with potting mix. Place the African milk tree in the center of the container and ensure it sits just below the rim. For this project, the plants should be placed right at rim level, instead of the typical 1 to 2 inches (2.5 to 5 cm) below the rim, so that the stonecrop looks as though it's overflowing from the container.

2. Add soil until it is 2 inches (5 cm) below the rim of the planter. Use the stonecrop to cover the soil around the African milk tree, leaving no gaps.

3. Water in the plants.

Note: *Always wear a pair of gloves when planting African milk tree. Its sap can irritate the skin.*

RECIPE 6

MID-CENTURY
CONCRETE

SEASONS: Spring through fall
LIGHT: Full sun
WATER: Moderate

———————

PLANTS

One 1-gallon (4 L) 'Barbeque' rosemary (*Rosmarinus officinalis*)

One 1-gallon (4 L) 'Yellow My Darling' coneflower (*Echinacea*)

One 4-inch (10 cm) common sage (*Salvia officinalis*)

Two 4-inch (5 cm) 'Silver Posie' variegated thymes (*Thymus vulgaris*)

CONTAINER & MATERIALS

14-inch-diameter (36 cm) concrete planter

Potting mix

1 Fill the container two-thirds of the way with potting mix. Place the rosemary at the back left side of the pot.

2 Place the coneflower next to the rosemary toward the back right side of the pot. Add more soil to the container so the smaller plants sit at the same level.

3 Plant the sage on the left side of the container. Place the variegated thymes in the front and right side of the container. Fill the gaps with soil and water in the plants.

SEASONS: Spring and summer
LIGHT: Full to partial sun
WATER: Moderate

———————

PLANTS

One 4-inch (10 cm) baby's tears (*Soleirolia soleirolii*)

One 4-inch (10 cm) purple trailing lantana (*Lantana montevidensis*)

One 4-inch (10 cm) 'Gold Nuggets' beggar-ticks (*Bidens ferulifolia*)

One 4-inch (10 cm) Iceland poppy (*Papaver nudicaule*)

CONTAINER & MATERIALS

12-inch-diameter (30 cm) white terrazzo planter

Potting mix

1 Fill the container three-quarters of the way with potting mix.

2 Place the baby's tears at the front edge of the container.

3 Add the lantana on the front left side of the container and the beggar-ticks toward the back of the container, just left of center. Add the Iceland poppy in the remaining hole. Fill the gaps with soil and water in the plants.

WHITE
TERRAZZO

HAND-BUILT CERAMIC

SEASONS: Spring through fall
LIGHT: Full sun to partial shade
WATER: Moderate

PLANTS

One 4-inch (10 cm) 'Hot Lips' salvia (*Salvia microphylla*)

One 4-inch (10 cm) 'Lemon Licorice' licorice plant (*Helichrysum petiolare*)

One 4-inch (10 cm) 'Cora Cascade Violet' vinca (*Catharanthus roseus*)

One 4-inch (10 cm) 'Compact Electric Orange' New Guinea impatiens (*Impatiens hawkeri*)

CONTAINER & MATERIALS

13-inch-diameter (33 cm) glazed ceramic planter

Potting mix

Quirky handmade pots like this one (from artist Cee Füllemann) need plants that match and complement their personality. The punchy red, orange, and pink flowers make the turquoise and lime splatter glaze pop!

1. Fill the container three-quarters of the way with potting mix. Place the salvia toward the back left side of the container.

2. Place the licorice plant at the front left side of the container.

3. Plant the vinca toward the front edge of the container.

4. Place the impatiens in the remaining space on the right side of the container.

5. Fill the gaps with soil and water in the plants.

Licorice Plant

PLANT TYPE: Treated as annual; tropical perennial in warmer climates

SEASONS: Spring through fall

LIGHT: Full to partial sun

WATER: Moderate

AVAILABLE COLORS: Silvery green, lime green, variegated

This plant is an absolute favorite of mine, for the effortless beauty it brings to any container garden. The licorice plant (*Helichrysum petiolare*) is a vigorous grower and comes in two versatile hues, a silvery gray-green and a lime green, each lending itself to a host of different design palettes. The small, round, velvety leaves have a tactile lure and beg to be touched. Very useful as a filler or spiller plant, it quickly covers any bare soil and gracefully trails down the sides of pots or hanging baskets. Its common name comes from its faint licorice scent, but it isn't related to the true licorice plant (*Glycyrrhiza glabra*), from which licorice extract is made, or other well-known licorice-flavored plants such as anise and fennel.

Licorice plant grows best in full sun to partial sun and is treated as an annual in cooler climates but will grow year-round in warmer zones. Once you try growing this plant, its ease and beauty will make you want to put it in every pot you plant.

CHECKERED FIBERGLASS

asparagus fern

*Captain Ventura
calla lily*

CHECKERED FIBERGLASS

SEASONS: Spring through fall
LIGHT: Full sun to partial shade
WATER: High

PLANTS

Two 1-gallon (4 L) Captain Ventura calla lilies (*Zantedeschia*)

One 4-inch (10 cm) asparagus fern (*Asparagus densiflorus*)

CONTAINER & MATERIALS

12-inch (30 cm) square painted fiberglass planter

Potting mix

Calla lilies exude drama with their long stems and tubular flowers. This variety has speckled leaves that complement the checkerboard pattern of the pot. The edges of the square vessel are softened by the fronds of the asparagus fern.

1. Fill the container halfway with potting mix. Place the calla lilies in the left and right corners of the container; this will fill up the bulk of the container, but be sure to leave a gap at the front corner.

2. Add more soil so the fern will sit at the same depth. Place the fern in the front corner of the pot. Fill the gaps with soil and water in the plants.

COLOR-DIPPED
CERAMIC

SEASONS: Spring and fall
LIGHT: Full to partial sun
WATER: High

———

PLANTS

Two 4-inch (10 cm) oxalis (*Oxalis triangularis*)

One 4-inch (10 cm) dusty miller (*Jacobaea maritima*)

One 4-inch (10 cm) Halios Select Victoria cyclamen (*Cyclamen persicum*)

CONTAINER & MATERIALS

10-inch-diameter (25 cm) glazed ceramic planter

Potting mix

1 Fill the container halfway with potting mix.

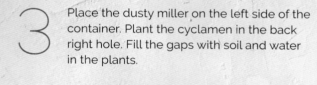

2 Place the two oxalis at the front of the container, slightly off center to the right.

3 Place the dusty miller on the left side of the container. Plant the cyclamen in the back right hole. Fill the gaps with soil and water in the plants.

CERAMIC TRIO

SEASONS: Spring through fall
LIGHT: Partial sun to partial shade
WATER: Moderate to high

PLANTS

One 5-gallon (19 L)
Xanadu philodendron
(*Thaumatophyllum xanadu*)

One 10-inch (25 cm) Pistachio
bigleaf hydrangea (*Hydrangea
macrophylla* 'Horwack')

Fourteen 2-inch (5 cm)
'Goldilocks' creeping Jennys
(*Lysimachia nummularia*)

One 4-inch (10 cm) 'Marmalade'
coralbells (*Heuchera*)

CONTAINERS & MATERIALS

16-inch-diameter (41 cm) white
ceramic fluted planter

12-inch-diameter (30 cm) white
textured ceramic planter

8-inch (20 cm) bell-shaped
glazed ceramic planter

Potting mix

Creating triangular groupings of containers is an almost foolproof way to come up with a pleasing arrangement. Although you'll want to be sure that all the plants in the grouping have similar light requirements, you can set pots with high water needs next to pots with low water needs, as long as you keep track of their various watering schedules. Smaller pots dry out faster than larger ones; in this grouping, the hydrangea has high water requirements and the smaller pot of coralbells and creeping Jenny will dry out faster than the large pot with the Xanadu philodendron, which has more moderate water needs.

1. Fill the largest pot one-third of the way with potting mix. Place the philodendron in the center of the container. Fill in around the plant with soil until it is even with the base of the plant.

2. Fill one-third of the medium-size pot with soil. Place the hydrangea toward the back of the container, leaving a gap of 2 to 3 inches (5 to 7.6 cm) around the front edge. Add soil so the creeping Jennys will sit at the same height as the hydrangea. Space six of the creeping Jennys around the front of the container. Fill the gaps with soil.

3. Fill the smallest container three-quarters of the way with soil. Place the coralbells in the center of the container. Add more soil around the plant so the creeping Jennys will sit at the same height as the coralbells. Evenly space the remaining eight creeping Jennys around the perimeter of the pot. Fill the gaps with soil and water in all three containers.

RECIPE 12

METALLIC-GLAZED CERAMIC

pink evening primrose

society garlic

Black Velvet
petunia

METALLIC-GLAZED CERAMIC

SEASONS: Spring through fall
LIGHT: Full sun
WATER: High

PLANTS

One 1-gallon (4 L) society garlic (*Tulbaghia violacea*)

Three 4-inch (10 cm) Black Velvet petunias (*Petunia × atkinsiana* 'Balpevac')

Two 4-inch (10 cm) pink evening primroses (*Oenothera speciosa*)

CONTAINER & MATERIALS

14-inch-diameter (36 cm) metallic-glazed ceramic planter

Potting mix

A contemporary twist on old-fashioned favorites: These sexy velvety black numbers aren't your grandma's petunias! This plant and pot combination is all about using tonal and textural opposites. I've paired the black petunias with the pale blooms of evening primrose and society garlic for a high-contrast pop. The velvety petals of the petunia stand out against the shiny metallic planter. Deadhead the flowers often to keep the plants blooming all season long.

1. Fill the container three-quarters of the way with potting mix. Place the society garlic in the center of the pot.

2. Add more soil to the container so that the smaller plants will sit at the same depth. Plant one petunia toward the front center and the other two on the back right and left sides.

3. Set the evening primroses in the holes on the front right and left sides. Fill the gaps with soil and water in the plants.

WOODEN BARREL

SEASONS: Summer and fall
LIGHT: Full sun
WATER: Moderate

————————

PLANTS

One 4-inch (10 cm) 'Cosmic
Eye' tickseed (*Coreopsis*)

One 4-inch (10 cm) 'Strictus'
eulalia (*Miscanthus sinensis*)

Two 4-inch (10 cm) Lascar Dark Red
verbenas (*Verbena* 'KLEVP12446')

Three 2-inch (5 cm) oxeye daisies
(*Leucanthemum vulgare*)

CONTAINER & MATERIALS

12-inch-diameter (30 cm) wooden barrel

Potting mix

1 Fill the container three-quarters of the way
with potting mix. Place the tickseed at the
front center of the barrel, 2 to 3 inches (5 to
7.6 cm) from the rim.

2 Place the eulalia toward the back center of
the barrel, directly behind the tickseed..

3 Add the verbenas, one toward the front
right and one toward the back left of the
barrel. Line the oxeye daisies up along
the front rim, starting at the left side and
abutting the verbena in the front right. Fill
the gaps with soil and water in the plants.

Tickseed

A profuse bloomer, tickseed (also called coreopsis, from its genus name, *Coreopsis*) is a must-grow plant for the flower lover who can't resist clipping a few, or even a handful, of stems to bring inside! Tickseed plants are also an excellent choice for long-lasting color in your container garden, where they bring a carefree and abundant feeling thanks to their narrow leaves, almost feathery-looking foliage, and bountiful flowers that stand tall or spill out of their pots. These plants lend themselves to naturalistic or cottage garden design (an informal style of dense planting that mixes decorative plants with edibles).

Nicknamed tickseed for the shape of its seeds, this wildflower comes in many varieties. Most are perennials, some are annuals—but all perform well in containers. When planted in the ground, they are drought tolerant, but in containers they require more frequent watering. They thrive in full sun and benefit from deadheading to keep their daisy-like flowers blooming through the seasons. If plants start looking long and leggy late in the season, prune them back two-thirds to encourage new growth.

PLANT TYPE: Perennial or annual, depending on variety

SEASONS: Early summer through fall

LIGHT: Full sun

WATER: Moderate

AVAILABLE COLORS: Yellow, gold, red, pink, orange, bicolor

FIBERGLASS
ORB

SEASONS: All
LIGHT: Partial sun
WATER: Low

PLANTS

One 6-inch (15 cm) aloe vera (*Aloe vera*)

One 6-inch (15 cm) fishhooks
(*Senecio radicans*)

One 6-inch (15 cm) burro's tail
(*Sedum morganianum*)

One 4-inch (10 cm) 'Ruby Slippers'
echeveria (*Echeveria harmsii*)

CONTAINER & MATERIALS

20-inch-diameter (51 cm) black planter

Succulent and cactus potting mix

Note: *In climates where temperatures
drop below 40°F (4°C), bring the planter
inside over winter.*

1 Fill the container three-quarters of the way with potting mix. Place the aloe vera at the back center of the pot.

2 Place the fishhooks on the right side of the container, draping the trails over the side of the pot.

3 Handling the plant by its root-ball, gently place the burro's tail at the front of the container, slightly to the left. Try not to touch the leaves, as they are easily knocked off. Fit the ruby slippers in the remaining hole on the left side of the pot. Fill the gaps with soil and water in the plants.

LARGE MINIMAL TERRA-COTTA

SEASONS: Spring through fall
LIGHT: Full sun
WATER: High

PLANTS

One 3-gallon (11 L) 'Red King Humbert' canna lily (*Canna*)

Two 6-inch (15 cm) 'Vancouver Centennial' geraniums (*Pelargonium × hortorum*)

One 6-inch (15 cm) asparagus fern (*Asparagus densiflorus*)

One 4-inch (10 cm) 'Lemon Licorice' licorice plant (*Helichrysum petiolare*)

CONTAINER & MATERIALS

A few curved crocks or rocks

20-inch-diameter (51 cm) terra-cotta planter

Potting mix

Welcome the feeling of a warm tropical breeze with this vibrant arrangement. The hot orange-red of the large canna lily flowers complements the small firecracker-like coral blooms of the geranium. The fiery flowers pop against the dark foliage and provide contrast against the bright greens of the asparagus fern and the licorice plant. The terra-cotta planter blends with the color palette and grounds the arrangement.

1. Place the crocks or rocks over the drainage hole of the planter and fill the container one-third of the way with potting mix.

2. Plant the canna lily at the back center of the container, then hold the plant in place by adding more soil until the container is two-thirds full.

3. Plant the two geraniums to the left side and front of the container. Add or remove soil as needed so that the crowns of these plants sit at the same height as the canna lily.

4. Place the asparagus fern in front of the canna lily, slightly offset to the right.

5. Add 3 inches (8 cm) of soil, or enough so that the licorice plant will sit at the same height as the rest of the plants. Place it toward the right edge of the container, with its leaves trailing over the sides. Fill the gaps with soil and water in the plants.

SEASON: Fall
LIGHT: Full sun
WATER: Moderate

———

PLANTS

One 1-gallon (4 L) 'Jade Princess'
ornamental millet (*Pennisetum glaucum*)

One 4-inch (10 cm) 'Profusion
Orange' zinnia (*Zinnia elegans*)

One 4-inch (10 cm) 'Cosmic
Eye' tickseed (*Coreopsis*)

One 4-inch (10 cm) 'Songbird White'
ornamental kale (*Brassica oleracea*)

CONTAINER & MATERIALS

12-inch (30 cm) square terra-cotta planter

Potting mix

1   Fill the container halfway with potting mix.
    Place the millet in the back corner of the
    planter.

2   Add more soil, then place the zinnia toward
    the right corner of the container so it sits at
    the same level.

3   Place the tickseed in the left corner. Plant
    the kale in the front corner, angled slightly
    forward, so it faces out and not directly up.
    Fill the gaps with soil and water in the plants.

SQUARE
TERRA-COTTA

2

WINDOW BOXES & TROUGHS

Window boxes and troughs are long, narrow containers designed for mounting under windows, fitting in tight spots, or adorning an outdoor dining table. These containers are particularly useful for adding curb appeal to your home by bringing liveliness and color.

Choosing a lightweight window box is helpful if you intend to mount it to siding or a railing. Always be sure to properly secure any suspended planter because soil and water will add significant weight.

Since window boxes are often viewed at a distance, look for bright and bold plants. Small troughs are excellent for tabletop arrangements. Select plants with low profiles so they don't impede conversation. Larger troughs are great for dividing space. They are deep enough to support bigger plants and provide height without a huge footprint.

COPPER
WINDOW BOX

SEASON: Spring
LIGHT: Partial sun to partial shade
WATER: High

———————

PLANTS

Two 1-gallon (4 L) 'Pacific Frost' Corsican hellebores (*Helleborus argutifolius*)

Two 4-inch (10 cm) Odessa Orange Bling Bling carnations (*Dianthus caryophyllus* 'Hilorbli')

Two 4-inch (10 cm) Piccadilly Dark Salmon twinspurs (*Diascia* 'KLEDB18008')

Two 4-inch (10 cm) 'Beacon Silver' spotted dead nettles (*Lamium*)

CONTAINER & MATERIALS

30-inch-long (76 cm) copper window box

Potting mix

1   Fill the container halfway with potting mix and plant the two hellebores in the center. Hellebores have sensitive roots, so take care to not disturb them. Add a layer of soil to hold them in place and so that the smaller plants will sit at the same level as the hellebores.

2   Set the carnations on either side of the hellebores, toward the back of the container.

3   Plant two twinspurs in front of the carnations, at the lip of the trough. Finally, plant the dead nettles on the outside edges of the container. Fill the gaps with soil and water in the plants.

Hellebores

Hellebores have a dark past and lore surrounding them. Not only does *hellebore* sound awfully close to *hell*, but the Greek name *Helleborus* translates to "injury food," hinting at its historical use by ancient herbalists and medieval witches for concocting poisons and casting malicious spells. These days, hellebores are a welcome addition to a container garden as one of the few cool-weather flowers whose blooms brighten shady spaces from winter through spring. During the coldest weather, place potted hellebores in a location where they will receive some dappled sunlight, and move the pots to a shady spot when the weather warms up. Be sure to plant in a container that can withstand freezing temperatures, such as one made from wood or fiberglass.

There are many varieties of hellebores, with blooms in hues from dark burgundy to bright white, each with its own charm. I particularly love 'Pacific Frost' for its mottled foliage and new growth that has a pink blush. Its blooms shift from creamy white to a vibrant green as they age. The sturdy stems also have a pink hue. The flowers gently hang their heads, so they are perfect for viewing from below, such as in a window box. One tip when planting hellebores is to be gentle with the roots, as they don't like to be disturbed. And be extra careful growing this "injury food" if you have curious pets or children.

PLANT TYPE: Perennial

SEASONS: Winter and spring

LIGHT: Partial shade to sun

WATER: High

AVAILABLE COLORS: Pale green, white, cream, burgundy, pink

MINIMAL
WINDOW BOX

Kiss Rose treasure flower

'Siskiyou Blue' fescue —————————————

'Fairy Dust Pink'
cuphea

'Nigrescens'
black mondo grass

MINIMAL WINDOW BOX

SEASONS: Spring through fall
LIGHT: Full sun
WATER: Moderate

PLANTS

One 4-inch (10 cm) 'Fairy Dust Pink' cuphea (*Cuphea ramosissima*)

Four 2-inch (5 cm) 'Siskiyou Blue' fescues (*Festuca idahoensis*)

Two 2-inch (5 cm) 'Nigrescens' black mondo grasses (*Ophiopogon planiscapus*)

Five 2-inch (5 cm) Kiss Rose treasure flowers (*Gazania rigens*)

CONTAINER & MATERIALS

16-inch-long (41 cm) composite window box

Potting mix

Create a splash with minimal effort thanks to showy treasure flowers and the prolific blooms that cover the cuphea from spring through fall. The light and dark grasses provide an airy frame for the flowering plants. Deadhead the treasure flowers when they begin to fade to encourage new blooms.

1. Fill the container three-quarters of the way with potting mix. Place the cuphea at the back center of the planter.

2. Add 1 to 2 inches (2.5 to 5 cm) of soil. Place two of the fescues next to the cuphea. Plant the other two fescues near the front left and right corners of the container.

3. Plant the black mondo grasses near the back left and right corners of the container.

4. Place the treasure flowers across the front edge of the container, spaced about 1 to 2 inches (2.5 to 5 cm) apart, in between the fescues. Fill the gaps with soil and water in the plants.

CONCRETE TROUGH

SEASONS: Summer and fall
LIGHT: Full sun
WATER: High

PLANTS

One 6-inch (15 cm) 'Sungold' cherry tomato (*Solanum lycopersicum*)

Four 4-inch (10 cm) 'Dark Opal' purple basils (*Ocimum basilicum*)

Two 4-inch (10 cm) bush basils (*Ocimum minimum*)

CONTAINER & MATERIALS

30-inch-long (76 cm) concrete trough

Potting mix

Pebbles

Tomato and basil are as welcome a pairing in your garden as they are on your plate: they share the same soil, water, and light requirements, and the strong scent of basil works to repel pests from your juicy tomatoes! Adding a layer of pebbles on top of the soil will help keep it moist and warm (since the stones not only prevent evaporation but also absorb heat from the sun), which tomatoes and basil love, giving your plants a jump-start before the weather is hot.

1. Fill the container halfway with potting mix. Place the tomato in the center of the planter. Add more soil so that the stem of the tomato plant is buried 1 to 2 inches (2.5 to 5 cm) below the top of the soil.

2. Place one purple basil plant at each corner of the container. Be sure not to plant them too close to the edges of the container, as you'll want to allow space for them to grow.

3. Plant the two bush basil plants, one in front of the tomato and one behind. Fill the gaps with soil and cover with a thin layer of pebbles. Water in the plants.

RECIPE 20

FIBER-CONCRETE TROUGH

purple coneflower

'Morello'
hummingbird mint

'Sea Shells Mix'
cosmos

FIBER-CONCRETE TROUGH

SEASONS: Spring through fall
LIGHT: Full sun
WATER: Moderate

PLANTS

Two 1-gallon (4 L) purple coneflowers (*Echinacea purpurea*)

Three 4-inch (10 cm) 'Sea Shells Mix' cosmos (*Cosmos bipinnatus*)

Two 4-inch (10 cm) 'Morello' hummingbird mints (*Agastache*)

CONTAINER & MATERIALS

A few curved crocks or rocks

30-inch-long (76 cm), 36-inch-tall (91 cm) fiber-concrete trough

Potting mix

Soften a modern planter with free-flowing and long-flowering cottage garden plants, such as cosmos, hummingbird mint, and purple coneflower. These blooms will attract a wide array of pollinators, including songbirds, hummingbirds, bees, and all sorts of flying insects. To keep them blooming until the weather gets cold, deadhead spent flowers often. At the end of the season, let the cosmos and coneflowers go to seed. These provide a yummy treat for the birds, and you can save some seeds for growing next year.

1. Place the crocks or rocks over the drainage hole of the trough. Fill the container three-quarters of the way with potting mix. Place the two coneflowers in the center of the trough, 2 to 3 inches (5 to 7.6 cm) apart.

2. Add more soil to the container so the smaller plants will sit at the same height. Space the three cosmos across the front of the container.

3. Plant the hummingbird mints on either end of the container. Fill the gaps with soil and water in the plants.

GLAZED CERAMIC TROUGH

SEASONS: Spring through fall
LIGHT: Full sun
WATER: Moderate

PLANTS

One 1-gallon (4 L) kangaroo paw (*Anigozanthos flavidus*)

Two 6-inch (15 cm) Latin American fleabanes (*Erigeron karvinskainus*)

Two 4-inch (10 cm) Ruby Glow spurges (*Euphorbia amygdaloides* 'Waleuphglo')

CONTAINER & MATERIALS

12-inch-long (30 cm) blue glazed ceramic trough

Potting mix

This low-maintenance planting boasts showy flowers and foliage that charm from late spring through fall. The kangaroo paw's sculptural inflorescence fans out into fuzzy red and yellow flowers, and these colors are picked up in the foliage of the spurge and the flowers of the fleabane. Instead of deadheading each fleabane flower as it finishes, wait until the bulk of the flowers have bloomed and then cut the plant back by one-third to encourage a second flush of blossoms. In mild climates, cut back the fleabane all the way to the soil in the fall and new growth will emerge in the spring.

1. Fill the bottom quarter of the trough with potting mix. Place the kangaroo paw toward the back center of the pot.

2. Place the two fleabanes along the front edge of the container. Add more soil so the smaller plants will sit at the same height.

3. Plant the two spurges on either side of the kangaroo paw. Fill the gaps with soil and water in the plants.

BOAT-SHAPED TROUGH

SEASON: Summer
LIGHT: Full to partial sun
WATER: High

———

PLANTS

Two clumps water hyacinth
(*Pontederia crassipes*)

One large and three small water
lettuces (*Pistia stratiotes*)

Three parrot's feathers
(*Myriophyllum aquaticum*)

Small amount duckweed
(*Lemna minor*)

CONTAINER

24-inch-long (61 cm) concrete
trough with no drain holes

Mix up the traditional tabletop arrangement by using water plants in a boat-shaped concrete trough. The water hyacinth's exquisite purplish-blue flowers with yellow teardrop markings last only a few days, blooming from mid- to late summer. These plants multiply quickly and will need to be transplanted to a larger pot (or thin the plants and add the discarded stems to a compost pile). Both the water hyacinth and parrot's feathers are invasive in natural bodies of water in many states, so always keep them confined to containers.

1. Fill your container three-quarters of the way with dechlorinated water (tap water that contains chlorine can damage the roots and kill off beneficial bacteria that nourish the plants). Place the two water hyacinth clumps in the center of the trough.

2. Place one large and one small water lettuce on the left side of the hyacinths and the two remaining small water lettuces on the right edge of the container.

3. Add the three parrot's feathers between the water hyacinth and the small water lettuces.

4. Sprinkle the duckweed around all parts of the container, letting it float on the surface of the water.

Note: *Water plants can't survive on water alone—add an aquatic fertilizer to keep them healthy, following the dilution ratio on the label.*

PLANT TYPE: Perennial in Zones 8 to 10; treated as annual in cooler climates

SEASON: Summer

LIGHT: Full to partial sun

WATER: High

AVAILABLE COLORS: Purple

Water Hyacinth

Water hyacinth (*Pontederia crassipes*) is an intriguing plant. Its bulbous base keeps it afloat, and its waxy leaves grow in a unique rosette shape. The flower spikes rise from the center of the rosette, each one with multiple tightly stacked blooms of purple flowers that have a distinctive yellow teardrop on the top petal. While the flowers are short-lived, their beauty is worth adding to your water container garden and the verdant foliage holds interest when the flowers are not in bloom. Look for water hyacinth at a local nursery that sells aquatic plants.

Native to the tropical climate of the Amazon basin in South America, water hyacinth is easy to grow, reproducing quickly by sending out runner stems from its base. This ease of reproduction causes ecological destruction and economic disruption when the plants block out light and choke oxygen in natural bodies of water, thus destroying habitat and biodiversity and clogging lakes, rivers, and other waterways. In fact, water hyacinth has been called the world's worst aquatic weed. For the home gardener, this means it is extremely important to grow the plant only in containers or in small man-made ponds where it cannot spread into the surrounding environment. Some states prohibit the sale of water hyacinth. Significant efforts have been made to remove it from natural bodies of water, but it continues to be a threat. However, interesting research is being done on its use as an organic fertilizer, and it has been used as feed for domestic animals because of its high protein and mineral content.

To keep visual balance in your small container garden, you will need to thin out the water hyacinth frequently. Offshoots can easily be snipped off where the runners are connected. If the plant's hairy roots have become too dense, give them a snip as well to help divide the plants. The offshoots can be tossed into your compost pile.

SEASON: Fall
LIGHT: Full sun
WATER: Moderate

———————

PLANTS

Three 4-inch (10 cm) Serenity Red African daisies (*Osteospermum ecklonis* 'Balsered')

Two 4-inch (10 cm) New Zealand irises (*Libertia peregrinans*)

Three 4-inch (10 cm) lamb's-ears (*Stachys byzantina*)

Six 2-inch (5 cm) pot marigolds (*Calendula officinalis*)

Three 4-inch (10 cm) 'Zwartkop' black rose aeoniums (*Aeonium arboreum*)

3 orange and 2 white mini pumpkins

CONTAINER & MATERIALS

36-inch-long (91 cm) metal table trough

Potting mix

1 Fill the bottom of the container with a thin layer of potting mix. Evenly space the three African daisies across the trough, leaving room on either end. Place the two irises between the daisies, leaving space between the plants.

2 Place the lamb's-ears to the right of each African daisy. Add more soil so the smallest plants will sit at the same level.

3 Starting at the right front corner and working your way to the back left corner, plant a zigzag of pot marigolds diagonally across the container. Space the three aeoniums across the front center edge. Fill the gaps with soil and water in the plants. Finally, place the pumpkins throughout the container, covering any bare soil.

LONG TABLE TROUGH

TRADITIONAL
WINDOW BOX

SEASONS: Fall through spring
LIGHT: Full sun
WATER: High

———————

PLANTS

Three 1-gallon (4 L) 'Totem' dwarf Italian cypresses (*Cupressus sempervirens*)

Four 4-inch (10 cm) dusty millers (*Jacobaea maritima*)

Two 4-inch (10 cm) white cyclamens (*Cyclamen persicum*)

Ten 2-inch (5 cm) Penny 'Red Blotch' pansies (*Viola cornuta*)

Four 2-inch (5 cm) Panola XP White pansies (*Viola × wittrockiana* 'PAS702648')

CONTAINER & MATERIALS

36-inch-long (91 cm) white window box

Potting mix

1 Fill the container halfway with potting mix. Space the three cypress trees out evenly across the container, leaving room on each side.

2 Add more soil to the container so that the dusty miller will sit at the same depth. Plant the four dusty millers along the back of the container, one at each corner and one peeking out between each tree.

3 Place the cyclamens toward the front edge of the container, in the spaces between the trees. Add more soil to the container so the smaller plants sit at the same level. Plant the pansies, alternating colors, across the front of the container in between the cyclamens. Fill the gaps with soil and water in the plants.

3

URNS

The urn has been a staple in formal gardens for centuries. In early Greek and Roman cultures, urns were most commonly made of marble or bronze. Later replicas were cast in concrete and iron in elaborate designs. Many urns today have a sleeker design, with clean lines and less ornamentation. Contemporary or classical, these containers literally put plants on a pedestal, elevating the arrangement into the center of attention. And many are statement pieces all on their own: set one as a focal point in the garden, or use a pair to flank a doorway for a grand entrance. Choosing plants that can stand up to the drama of the urn is an art unto itself. In this chapter, we look at the simplest designs, as well as ways to create exuberant, lush arrangements.

CLASSIC CONCRETE

SEASONS: Spring through fall
LIGHT: Full sun to partial shade
WATER: Moderate

———————

PLANTS

One 4-inch (10 cm) creeping Jenny
(*Lysimachia nummularia*)

One 4-inch (10 cm)
Spotlight Lime Heart sweet potato vine
(*Ipomoea batatas* 'Balspotimart')

One 4-inch (10 cm) silver lady
fern (*Blechnum gibbum*)

One 4-inch (10 cm) 'Scarlet Flame'
caladium (*Caladium hortulanum*)

CONTAINER & MATERIALS

10-inch-diameter (25 cm) concrete urn

Potting mix

1 Fill the urn about three-quarters full with potting mix. Place the creeping Jenny off-center toward the left side of the urn, with the leaves spilling down the side. Add the sweet potato vine toward the front of the urn next to the creeping Jenny.

2 Place the silver lady fern toward the back of the urn, opposite the creeping Jenny.

3 Add the caladium for a punch of colorful foliage. Fill the gaps with soil and water in the plants.

Caladium

A classic choice for container gardens, plants from the *Caladium* genus are known for their fabulous heart-shaped foliage in brilliant patterns of red, pink, white, and green. They add color to shady spots in the garden, though many cultivars have been bred to tolerate sun. Caladiums are bold enough to make a statement all on their own, but they also work well as a colorful focal plant in mixed arrangements. Caladiums grow from tubers and love warm, humid climates. They go dormant when the days cool. If you live in Zones 9 to 11, you can plant them in the ground or leave them in the container over winter, but in climates where the ground freezes, they should be treated as annuals or stored inside in a cool, dark place and planted out when the danger of frost has passed.

PLANT TYPE: Perennial

SEASONS: Spring through fall

LIGHT: Shade to full sun

WATER: Moist, but not soggy

AVAILABLE COLORS: Green, pink, white, red

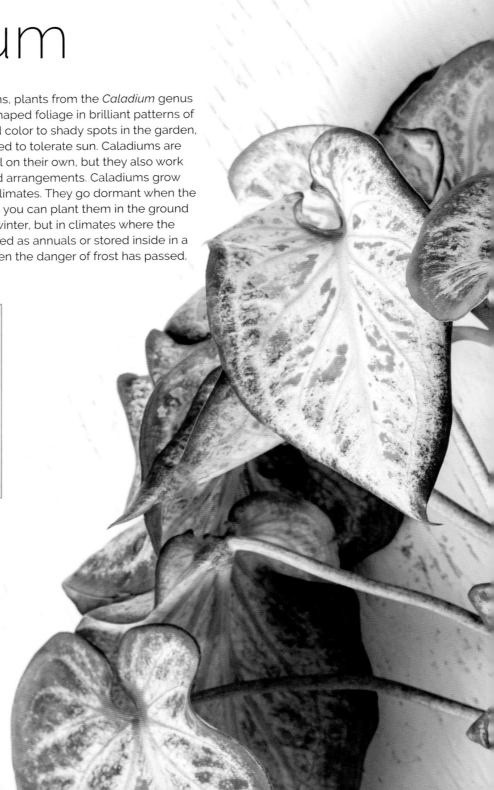

VINTAGE PAINTED IRON

SEASON: Spring
LIGHT: Full sun
WATER: High

PLANTS

One 2-gallon (8 L) 'Camelot Lavender' foxglove (*Digitalis purpurea*)

Two 4-inch (10 cm) red-veined sorrels (*Rumex sanguineus*)

Two 4-inch (10 cm) 'Palace Purple' coralbells (*Heuchera micrantha*)

CONTAINER & MATERIALS

Sphagnum moss

14-inch-diameter (36 cm) painted metal urn

Potting mix

Foxglove's towering flower spikes make a dramatic addition to a spring container. Deadhead spent flowers to encourage a second round of blooms. When buying flowering plants from your local nursery, look for those with many unopened buds and lots of healthy foliage. Here purple coralbells and red sorrel echo the color of the freckles inside the foxglove's tubular flowers, visually tying the arrangement together.

1. Soak the moss in water for a few minutes until it is soft, then wring out the excess moisture. Line the urn with a 2-inch-thick (5 cm) layer of moss to hold the soil in the container, so it doesn't wash out when you water. Fill the urn halfway with potting mix.

2. Place the foxglove toward the back center of the urn. Add more soil so the smaller plants will sit at the same height as the foxglove.

3. Alternate the sorrels and coralbells around the front of the urn. Fill the gaps with soil and top off the container with a thin layer of sphagnum moss, to act as a mulch to keep the soil moist between waterings. Water in the plants.

WOVEN METAL

SEASONS: Spring and summer
LIGHT: Partial sun
WATER: Moderate

PLANTS

One 1-gallon (4 L) 'Red Hobbit' columbine (*Aquilegia*)

Two 4-inch (10 cm) 'Heart and Soul' caladiums (*Caladium hortulanum*)

One 4-inch (10 cm) 'Gold Dust' English ivy (*Hedera helix*)

One 4-inch (10 cm) variegated yellow archangel (*Lamium galeobdolon* 'Variegatum')

CONTAINER & MATERIALS

13-inch-diameter (33 cm) woven metal urn

Spanish moss (*Tillandsia usneoides*)

Potting mix

1 Line the urn with a 2-inch-thick (5 cm) layer of moss. This will hold the soil in the container. Fill the urn three-quarters of the way with potting mix, then set the columbine in the center of the urn, so it sits an inch (2.5 cm) below the rim.

2 Place the caladiums on either side of the columbine, adding enough soil under them so that they sit at the same height as the columbine.

3 Plant the ivy on the right side of the urn and the yellow archangel on the left, and fill in the gaps with soil. Top off the planting with another layer of Spanish moss, to act as a mulch to keep the soil moist between waterings. Water in the plants.

MODERN CONCRETE

'Turquoise Tails'
stonecrop

'Crinoline Ruffles'
echeveria

'Blue Pearl' sedum

MODERN CONCRETE

SEASONS: All

LIGHT: Full to partial sun

WATER: Low

PLANTS

One 4-inch (10 cm) 'Blue Pearl' sedum (*Hylotelephium*)

One 4-inch (10 cm) 'Turquoise Tails' stonecrop (*Petrosedum sediforme*)

Two 4-inch (10 cm) 'Crinoline Ruffles' echeverias (*Echeveria*)

CONTAINER & MATERIALS

12-inch-diameter (30 cm) white concrete urn

Succulent and cactus potting mix

This arrangement spotlights the different textures, colors, and growth habits found in the succulent family. Though succulents are known for their thick, fleshy foliage, here it's the impressive inflorescences of the echeverias that really steal the show. Tall pink spikes shoot out from between the leaves and end with an arching cascade of ten or more flowers that open one after the other. After the flowers fade, trim back the spike as close to the plant as possible for a tidy look. In mild climates, succulents can stay outside year-round, but if temperatures dip below 40°F (4°C), bring them inside to overwinter.

1. Fill the container three-quarters of the way with potting mix. Set the 'Blue Pearl' sedum toward the back left edge of the container.

2. Place the 'Turquoise Tails' stonecrop at the front left side of the container, so that the stems spill over the edge.

3. Plant the right side of the container with the two echeverias. Fill the gaps with soil and water in the plants.

TRADITIONAL

SEASONS: Spring through fall
LIGHT: Partial sun to shade
WATER: High

PLANTS

One 1-gallon (4 L) umbrella
papyrus (*Cyperus alternifolius*)

One 6-inch (15 cm) 'Regal Shields'
elephant ear (*Alocasia*)

One 6-inch (15 cm) Boston
fern (*Nephrolepis exaltata*)

One 4-inch (10 cm) 'Black Beauty'
taro (*Colocasia esculenta*)

CONTAINER & MATERIALS

18-inch-diameter (46 cm)
fiberglass urn

Potting mix

This lush arrangement is all about the foliage: a classic Boston fern gets a little tropical flair when paired with papyrus and elephant ear plants. There are no flowers in this arrangement, but there is plenty of variety and visual interest thanks to the different textures and forms of foliage: the bright green, dense fern fronds contrast with the papyrus's tall, bare stems that end in bursts of narrow leaves, both of which are strikingly different from the dark, velvety, broad leaves of the elephant ear and the taro.

1. Fill the urn three-quarters of the way with potting mix. Place the papyrus toward the back right side of the container. Add more soil to the container so the next plant will sit at the same height.

2. Place the elephant ear to the left of the papyrus at the back left side of the container.

3. Plant the Boston fern at the front of the container, slightly offset to the left, so that its arching fronds spill over the edge. Add more soil so the smallest plant, the taro, will sit at the same level. Tuck the taro between the fern and the papyrus. Fill the gaps with soil and water in the plants.

CONTEMPORARY HOURGLASS

SEASONS: Spring through fall
LIGHT: Full sun
WATER: Moderate

PLANTS

One 1-gallon (4 L) Serenity Coral Magic African daisy (*Osteospermum ecklonis* 'Balsercoric')

One 5-inch (13 cm) 'Red Sister' ti plant (*Cordyline fruticosa*)

One 4-inch (10 cm) Lava Rose coleus (*Plectranthus scutellarioides* 'Kakegawa CE1')

One 4-inch (10 cm) Pazzaz Tangerine purslane (*Portulaca oleracea*)

CONTAINER & MATERIALS

12-inch-diameter (30 cm) blue hourglass planter

Potting mix

1 Fill the container halfway with soil. Place the African daisy toward the front left edge of the container.

2 Add more soil so the next plants will sit at the same level. Set the ti plant at the back left side of the container.

3 Add more soil to the container. Place the coleus on the right edge slightly toward the back of the container. In the space at the front right side of the container, plant the purslane. Fill the gaps with soil and water in the plants.

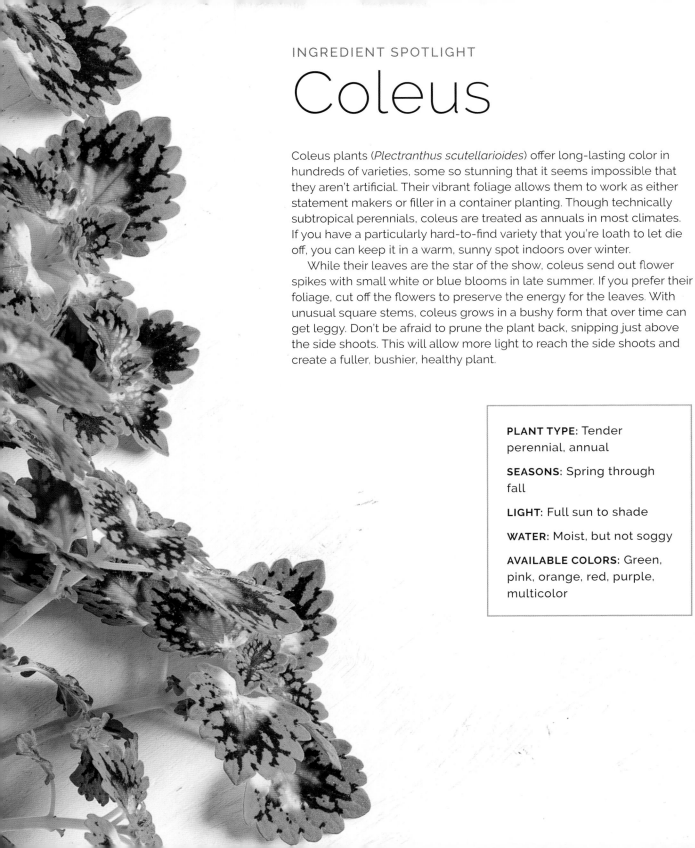

Coleus

Coleus plants (*Plectranthus scutellarioides*) offer long-lasting color in hundreds of varieties, some so stunning that it seems impossible that they aren't artificial. Their vibrant foliage allows them to work as either statement makers or filler in a container planting. Though technically subtropical perennials, coleus are treated as annuals in most climates. If you have a particularly hard-to-find variety that you're loath to let die off, you can keep it in a warm, sunny spot indoors over winter.

While their leaves are the star of the show, coleus send out flower spikes with small white or blue blooms in late summer. If you prefer their foliage, cut off the flowers to preserve the energy for the leaves. With unusual square stems, coleus grows in a bushy form that over time can get leggy. Don't be afraid to prune the plant back, snipping just above the side shoots. This will allow more light to reach the side shoots and create a fuller, bushier, healthy plant.

PLANT TYPE: Tender perennial, annual

SEASONS: Spring through fall

LIGHT: Full sun to shade

WATER: Moist, but not soggy

AVAILABLE COLORS: Green, pink, orange, red, purple, multicolor

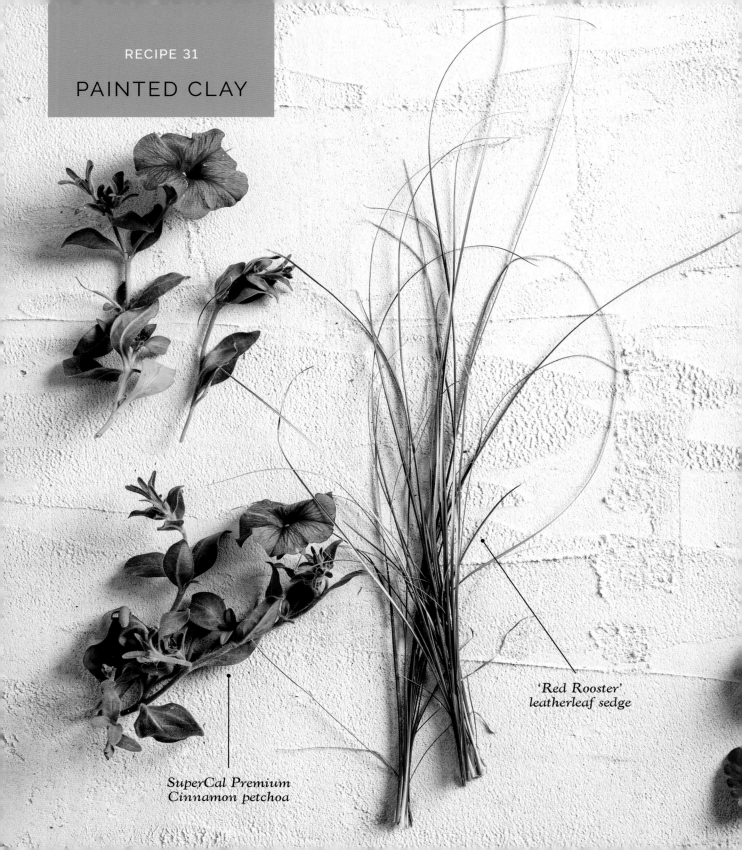

PAINTED CLAY

SuperCal Premium
Cinnamon petchoa

'Red Rooster'
leatherleaf sedge

*Frizzle Sizzle
Mini Yellow viola*

*Frizzle Sizzle
Orange pansy*

*Spotlight Red Heart
sweet potato vine*

PAINTED CLAY

SEASON: Fall
LIGHT: Full sun
WATER: High

PLANTS

One 4-inch (10 cm) 'Red Rooster' leatherleaf sedge (*Carex buchananii*)

One 4-inch (10 cm) Spotlight Red Heart sweet potato vine (*Ipomoea batatas* 'Balspotredart')

One 4-inch (10 cm) SuperCal Premium Cinnamon petchoa (*Petunia × Calibrachoa* 'SAKPXCO21')

One 4-inch (10 cm) Frizzle Sizzle Orange pansy (*Viola × wittrockiana*)

One 4-inch (10 cm) Frizzle Sizzle Mini Yellow viola (*Viola cornuta*)

CONTAINERS & MATERIALS

One 10-inch-diameter (25 cm) clay planter

One 8-inch-diameter (20 cm) clay planter

Potting mix

An easy trick for creating an elevated planter or urn is to simply place one pot on top of another. Featuring autumn colors, this planting combination will mature nicely through late fall as the potato vine and petchoa trail down the sides of the container.

1. Stack the 10-inch (25 cm) planter on top of the upside-down 8-inch (20 cm) planter. Fill the container three-quarters of the way with potting mix. Position the sedge toward the back center of the container.

2. Set the sweet potato vine on the left edge of the container and the petchoa on the right edge of the container, arranged so their leaves and flowers will trail down the sides.

3. At the front of the container, plant the pansy and viola next to each other. Fill the gaps with soil and water in the plants.

4

BOWLS

Bowls make fun low planters and can be a strategic addition to a grouping of other pots, where the goal is to have multiple levels of interest (for more on this, see page 30). A bowl's low profile also lends itself to tabletop centerpieces.

However you arrange them, bowls are often viewed from above, and they typically feature a large surface area. For that reason, you'll need to consider the bowl's top-down view and avoid leaving bare patches of soil. Several projects in this chapter use rocks or ground cover as intentional design elements.

Bowls present other unique challenges. If a bowl lacks drainage holes (a common situation), you'll need to drill some before planting. And due to the shallow depth, you'll need to choose plants with shallow roots—or deeper bowls to allow more space for roots. Most annuals have shallow roots, and other plants that have a fibrous root system (not a taproot that requires soil depth) are best for growing in bowls. You can tell the type of root system by popping a plant out of its pot. If the roots look like a fine mesh and are all roughly the same size, they are considered a fibrous root system; if there are distinct thick roots with smaller branching roots, it's a taproot system.

FLUTED CERAMIC

SEASONS: Spring through fall
LIGHT: Full sun
WATER: Moderate

PLANTS

One 1-gallon (4 L) Lucky
Star lavender star flower
(*Pentas lanceolata*)

One 4-inch (10 cm) 'Kent Beauty'
ornamental oregano (*Origanum*)

One 4-inch (10 cm) Delta Premium
True Blue pansy (*Viola × wittrockiana*)

One 4-inch (10 cm) 'Nagoya Red'
ornamental kale (*Brassica oleracea*)

CONTAINER & MATERIALS

12-inch-diameter (30 cm)
blue fluted ceramic bowl

Potting mix

Color and texture are the driving force behind this Impressionist painting–inspired arrangement. Your eyes dance around the container just as they would when viewing one of Monet's water lily paintings. This arrangement's soft spring palette of pinks and blues feels fresh thanks to the zippy chartreuse foliage of the 'Kent Beauty' oregano. Don't try to eat it: this ornamental-only oregano produces gorgeous pink-purple pendulous flowers. Deadhead the pansy and star flower as the blossoms fade to encourage more blooms.

1. Fill the container one-quarter of the way with potting mix. Place the star flower at the back center of the container.

2. Add 2 inches (5 cm) of soil. Plant the oregano on the right side of the container so its foliage angles outward.

3. Place the pansy at the front left side of the container so its flowers reach out over the edge.

4. Plant the kale at the front center, angled so it faces outward and not upward. Fill the gaps with soil and water in the plants.

RECIPE 33

GEOMETRIC TERRAZZO

'Limewire' coleus

fiber-optic grass

'Alabama Sunrise' foamy bells

'Big Leaf' creeping wire vine

GEOMETRIC TERRAZZO

SEASONS: Spring through fall
LIGHT: Partial sun to partial shade
WATER: High

PLANTS

One 1-gallon (4 L) 'Alabama Sunrise'
foamy bells (× *Heucherella*)

One 6-inch (15 cm) 'Limewire' coleus
(*Plectranthus scutellarioides*)

One 4-inch (10 cm) fiber-optic
grass (*Isolepis cernua*)

One 4-inch (10 cm) 'Big
Leaf' creeping wire vine
(*Muehlenbeckia complexa*)

CONTAINER & MATERIALS

14-inch-diameter (36 cm)
terrazzo hexagonal bowl

Potting mix

Color-temperature contrast is a great design element to incorporate into your arrangements. Cool colors are generally blues, purples, and greens, and warm colors are reds, oranges, and yellows. However, depending on the undertones, every color can lean warm or cool. This arrangement contrasts warm and cool colors by pairing a terrazzo planter in aqua—a cool color—with plants in a palette of warm yellows, deep reds, burgundies, and vibrant lime green. The combination is electric!

1. Fill the bowl halfway with potting mix. Set the foamy bells at the back of the container. Add another layer of soil to hold the root-ball in place.

2. Plant the coleus to the left front side of the bowl and add more soil to hold it in place.

3. Insert the fiber-optic grass and wire vine in the remaining space, with the wire vine spilling out and trailing down the front right side of the bowl. The thin leaves of the grass nicely contrast with the small round leaves on the wire vine. Fill the gaps with soil and water in the plants.

Coralbells

An all-star container and garden plant, coralbells (*Heuchera* species) boast colorful foliage and long-lasting blooms. The leaves can be ruffled, patterned, waxy, or smooth, in colors that range from vibrant yellows, reds, greens, oranges, and silvers to purples so deep they almost appear black. Some varieties' foliage even shifts colors as the leaves mature or when the weather changes. Many send out sturdy flower spikes with tiny bell-like flowers in shades from red to hot pink to white, giving the plant its common name, coralbells. These spikes can reach 1 to 3 feet (30.5 to 91 cm) tall and bloom for two to three weeks from late spring to summer, making them excellent cut flowers. Deadheading lengthens the flowering time by encouraging repeat blooms.

Native to forests of North America, these easy-to-grow and versatile plants can be kept in full sun or shade, but most are happiest in dappled light. Darker, more textured foliage tends to handle hot direct heat better than lighter, shiny-leafed varieties. Below Zone 6b, consider resettling the plants in the ground for winter, or protect the pots from freezing (see page 25). If the foliage looks a little tired after winter, cut it back to encourage fresh growth for spring.

PLANT TYPE: Evergreen perennial

SEASONS: Spring through fall

LIGHT: Full sun to shade

WATER: Moderate to high

AVAILABLE COLORS: Chartreuse, green, yellow, red, peach, orange, purple, silver, multicolor

RECIPE 34

LARGE TERRA-COTTA

SEASONS: Spring through fall
LIGHT: Partial shade to shade
WATER: High

PLANTS

One 3-gallon (11 L) variegated leopard plant (*Farfugium japonicum* 'Aureomaculatum')

Two 5-inch (13 cm) 'Tiger Paws' begonias (*Begonia*)

Two 4-inch (10 cm) Zinfandel oxalis (*Oxalis vulcanicola*)

CONTAINER & MATERIALS

24-inch-diameter (61 cm) terra-cotta bowl

Potting mix

This arrangement will brighten up a shady spot in your yard, with fun foliage and a mix of plants that will alternate blooming spring through fall. The star of the arrangement is the leopard plant with its eye-catching large waxy leaves. I prefer the variegated variety because the yellow spots add a focal point in the shade. Underplant it with 'Tiger Paws' begonia, which has equally interesting foliage with its green-and-brown mottled leaves and cute pink flowers that bloom in spring. The oxalis is a vigorous grower that will spill down the sides of the bowl and continuously bloom spring through summer with its little yellow flowers that pick up the yellow spots on the leopard plant. In fall, the leopard plant will send up daisy-like yellow flower spikes. Be sure to use a large bowl for this lush arrangement.

1. Fill the bottom third of the container with potting mix and place the leopard plant toward the back center of the pot. Add more soil around the plant until the container is two-thirds full.

2. Place the two begonias front and center. Be sure they are sitting at the same height as the leopard plant; if not, add more soil to raise them.

3. Plant the oxalis on either side of the begonias so they spill down the sides of the pot. Fill the gaps with soil and water in the plants.

CONTEMPORARY
FIBER CONCRETE

SEASONS: All
LIGHT: Full sun
WATER: Low

PLANTS

Two 1-gallon (4 L) cat tails euphorbias (*Euphorbia leucadendron*)

One 6-inch (15 cm) bunny ears cactus (*Opuntia microdasys*)

Two 4-inch (10 cm) 'Siskiyou Blue' fescues (*Festuca idahoensis*)

Three 4-inch (10 cm) Mexican feather grasses (*Nassella tenuissima*) (see Note)

CONTAINER & MATERIALS

20-inch-diameter (51 cm) fiber concrete bowl

Succulent and cactus potting mix

Note: *In California, Mexican feather grass is invasive. Substitute with Indian ricegrass (Stipa hymenoides) or nodding needle grass (Stipa cernua).*

1 Wear gloves for this recipe! The fuzzy hairs on the bunny ears cactus can make your skin very itchy. Fill the container halfway with potting mix. Place the two euphorbias toward the back of the bowl, slightly offset from each other on a diagonal. Add more soil to help hold them in place.

2 Place the bunny ears front and center, adding more soil around the base of the plant to hold it in place.

3 Add the two fescues on either side of the cactus. For a final touch, plant the Mexican feather grasses along the back right and back left edges of the container, with the euphorbia in between. These grasses bring an airiness to the rigid, dramatic silhouettes of the cacti. Fill the gaps with soil and water in the plants. If your temperatures dip below freezing, protect or bring inside for winter.

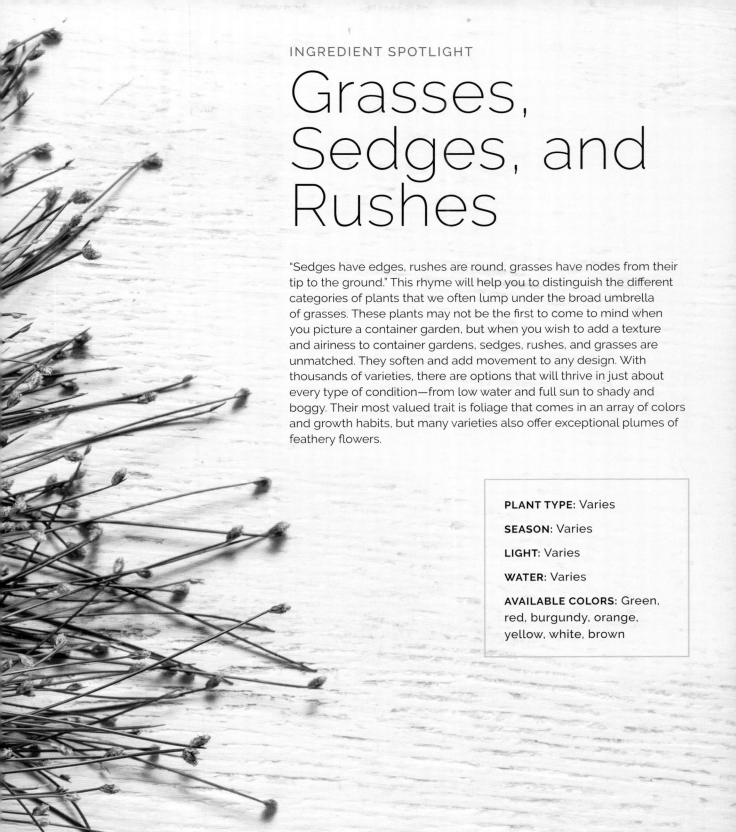

Grasses, Sedges, and Rushes

"Sedges have edges, rushes are round, grasses have nodes from their tip to the ground." This rhyme will help you to distinguish the different categories of plants that we often lump under the broad umbrella of grasses. These plants may not be the first to come to mind when you picture a container garden, but when you wish to add a texture and airiness to container gardens, sedges, rushes, and grasses are unmatched. They soften and add movement to any design. With thousands of varieties, there are options that will thrive in just about every type of condition—from low water and full sun to shady and boggy. Their most valued trait is foliage that comes in an array of colors and growth habits, but many varieties also offer exceptional plumes of feathery flowers.

PLANT TYPE: Varies

SEASON: Varies

LIGHT: Varies

WATER: Varies

AVAILABLE COLORS: Green, red, burgundy, orange, yellow, white, brown

CORTEN STEEL

SEASONS: Spring through fall
LIGHT: Partial sun to partial shade
WATER: High

PLANTS

One 1-gallon (4 L) dwarf
papyrus (*Cyperus isocladus*)

Eleven 4-inch (10 cm) golden
spikemoss (*Selaginella
kraussiana* 'Aurea')

CONTAINER & MATERIALS

22-inch-diameter (56 cm)
Corten steel bowl

Potting mix

Dark decorative pebbles

Mirrored forms are the goal of this arrangement. An airy papyrus creates a round dome, echoing the shape of the bowl. This circular theme is repeated in the electric ring of golden spikemoss, which contrasts starkly with the dark decorative rocks. This simple combination demonstrates that less is more.

1. Fill the bottom third of the container with potting mix. Place the papyrus in the center of the container.

2. Add soil so the smaller plants will sit at the same level as the papyrus. Plant the spikemoss in a ring around the papyrus, tightly spaced to leave no gaps. Space the plants about 2½ inches (6 cm) away from the rim of the bowl and from the papyrus's stems and root-ball.

3. Fill the gaps with soil. Top the soil with decorative pebbles, spreading them right up to the stems of the plants. Water in the plants.

SQUARE CERAMIC

SEASONS: Spring through fall
LIGHT: Partial sun to partial shade
WATER: High

———————

PLANTS

One 6-inch (15 cm) On Top 'Sun Glow'
tuberous begonia (*Begonia × tuberosa*)

One 6-inch (15 cm) autumn fern
(*Dryopteris erythrosora*)

One 4-inch (10 cm) Illusion Midnight Lace
sweet potato vine (*Ipomoea batatas*)

Four 4-inch (10 cm) Scotch moss
(*Arenaria verna* 'Aurea')

CONTAINER & MATERIALS

14-inch (36 cm) square glazed
ceramic bowl

Potting mix

1 Fill the container with potting mix so the begonia sits 2 inches (5 cm) below the rim. Plant the begonia in the back left corner.

2 Plant the autumn fern in the front left corner of the container. Add more soil so the smaller plants will sit at the same level in the container.

3 Place the sweet potato vine in the middle of the container; it will serve as a nice filler underneath the begonia. Use the four Scotch moss plants to cover the empty space in the front and right side of the container. Fill the gaps with soil and water in the plants.

GLAZED CERAMIC

SEASONS: Summer and fall
LIGHT: Full sun
WATER: Moderate

PLANTS

Two 4-inch (10 cm) sun balls
(*Craspedia globosa*)

Two 4-inch (10 cm) Talent Orange
treasure flowers (*Gazania rigens*)

Sixteen 2-inch (5 cm) silver
carpets (*Dymondia margaretae*)

CONTAINER & MATERIALS

12-inch-diameter (30 cm)
green glazed ceramic bowl

Potting mix

Approach this arrangement as if you're creating an abstract painting, with a dominant palette of cool silvery greens. The silver carpet is the unifying element, which blends with the glaze of the pot and the silvery gray-green foliage of the treasure flowers and sun balls. The plants' long, lyrical stems create negative space that is punctuated with hot bursts of yellow sun balls and vibrant orange open-faced treasure flowers.

1. Fill the container halfway with potting mix. Place the sun balls next to each other toward the back center of the container.

2. Plant the treasure flowers next to each other in front of the sun balls. Leave a little gap between the plants to allow room to grow.

3. Add 2 inches (5 cm) more soil. Fill in the remaining space around the perimeter of the bowl with the silver carpet plants. Fill in any small gaps with soil and water in the plants.

PLANTS

One 6-inch (15 cm) old man cactus
(*Cephalocereus senilis*)

One 3-inch (8 cm) panda plant
(*Kalanchoe tomentosa*)

Two 3-inch (8 cm) variegated lavender
scallops (*Kalanchoe fedtschenkoi* 'Variegata')

One 4-inch (10 cm) 'Blue Pearl'
sedum (*Hylotelephium*)

CONTAINER & MATERIALS

12-inch (30 cm) hand-built
ceramic glazed bowl

Succulent and cactus potting mix

1 Wear leather gloves for this recipe, as you'll be dealing with a cactus. Fill the container three-quarters of the way with potting mix and place the old man cactus at the back left. Add more soil to hold the cactus in place.

2 Place the panda plant at the front right edge of the container.

3 Place one of the lavender scallops at the front left edge and the other behind the panda plant. Place the sedum at the front center edge. Fill the gaps with soil and water in the plants.

TEXTURED CERAMIC

MID-CENTURY MODERN

white Iceland poppy

Cabaret Bright
Red calibrachoa

'Sparkling Burgundy'
coralbells

'Tomer Red'
Persian buttercup

parrot's beak

rosemary

MID-CENTURY MODERN

SEASONS: Late fall through spring
LIGHT: Full sun
WATER: Moderate

PLANTS

One 1-gallon (4 L) rosemary (*Rosmarinus officinalis*)

One 6-inch (15 cm) 'Sparkling Burgundy' coralbells (*Heuchera*)

Three 4-inch (10 cm) 'Tomer Red' Persian buttercups (*Ranunculus asiaticus*)

Two 4-inch (10 cm) white Iceland poppies (*Papaver nudicaule*)

Two 4-inch (10 cm) Cabaret Bright Red calibrachoas (*Calibrachoa × hybrida* 'Balacabrite')

Two 4-inch (10 cm) parrot's beaks (*Lotus berthelotii*)

CONTAINER & MATERIALS

24-inch-diameter (61 cm) black glazed ceramic bowl

Potting mix

Ring in the holiday season with this festive planting, or gift it in lieu of a bouquet come February 14. The strong vertical stems of rosemary and the deep red coralbells leaves anchor the planting. Crimson petals of the buttercups and calibrachoas and the paper-white blooms of the Iceland poppies dance across the arrangement, carrying the eye around the bowl. While these plants are available in nurseries during winter in areas of the country with mild climates, you might find them only in the fall and spring in colder zones.

1. Fill the bottom third of the container with potting mix. Place the rosemary toward the back right side of the bowl, leaving a gap between the root-ball and the rim.

2. Add more soil to the container so the coralbells will sit even with the rosemary. Place the coralbells in the center of the container next to the rosemary.

3. Add more soil to the entire bowl so that the 4-inch (10 cm) plants will sit at the same level as the other plants. Plant the buttercups, one at the back center edge, one at the right edge, and one toward the front right edge of the bowl.

4. Next plant the Iceland poppies, setting one on the left middle next to the coralbells and one in between the two buttercups on the right edge of the container. The long stems of the poppies and the flower spikes of the coralbells add nice linear movement and create negative space.

5. Plant the calibrachoas, one front and center and one on the left edge.

6. Finally, add the two parrot's beaks next to each other on the left front edge so their feathery foliage spills over the side of the bowl, softening the arrangement. Fill the gaps with soil and water in the plants.

5

HANGING BASKETS

Hanging baskets have unique, effortless charm, suspended in the air with their abundant flowers and plants spilling over the sides. However, achieving "effortlessness" takes a bit of attention and work! Because the baskets are often shallow or have a moss lining, they dry out quickly, so it's important to keep a close eye on them and water frequently.

Many hanging basket styles and materials are available. Metal wire versions are the most lightweight. (Skip the store-bought coco coir and elevate the look by lining your basket with moss, living or preserved.) Ceramic planters are heavier but won't dry out as quickly. Regardless of the container you choose, be sure the chain or straps are strong, use an anchor, and hang the container from a solid surface that can support the weight of the planter plus the added plants, soil, and water.

When thinking about hanging basket design, remember that these vessels are most often viewed from below, so choosing plants that cascade or stand out is key. In this chapter, we use a variety of containers that lend themselves to different design aesthetics, from contemporary to traditional, with plant combinations that accentuate each style.

SEASONS: Spring through fall
LIGHT: Full to partial sun
WATER: High

———————

PLANTS

Two 4-inch (10 cm) Superbells Grape Punch calibrachoas (*Calibrachoa × hybrida* 'JGCAL09404')

One 4-inch (10 cm) 'Riviera Midnight Blue' lobelia (*Lobelia erinus*)

One 4-inch (10 cm) 'Sentimental Blue' balloon flower (*Platycodon grandiflorus*)

One 4-inch (10 cm) Boston fern (*Nephrolepis exaltata*)

CONTAINER & MATERIALS

12-inch-diameter (30 cm) painted metal hanging basket with palm tree pattern

Sheet moss

Potting mix

1 Line the basket with sheet moss, slightly overlapping each piece so soil doesn't fall through the cracks. Fill the bottom half of the basket with potting mix. Place the two calibrachoas on the right edge of the basket.

2 Place the lobelia at the front left side of the container.

3 Plant the balloon flower at the back center edge of the basket. Add the fern, angled outward, at the back left side of the basket. Fill the gaps with soil and water in the plants.

SQUARE WIRE

SEASONS: Spring and summer
LIGHT: Partial shade
WATER: High

———

PLANTS

Forty-eight 2-inch (5 cm) Irish moss (*Sagina subulata*)

One 12-inch (30 cm) 'Seventh Heaven' giant fuchsia (*Fuchsia*)

Two 4-inch (10 cm) western sword ferns (*Polystichum munitum*)

CONTAINER & MATERIALS

14-inch (36 cm) square wire hanging basket

Potting mix

I love lining a hanging basket with living moss for the vibrance and mystery it brings to an arrangement. It requires a bit more work and watering but is worth the effort. When choosing a wire basket to hold a living moss liner, select one with small gaps between the wires to help prevent the moss from falling through the cracks. I prefer thin wires over thicker metal because the moss will hide the wires, especially as it grows, creating the illusion of a floating moss ball. In this design, the moss provides a striking green backdrop to the pendulous fuchsia flowers.

1. Pop out the moss from the cell packs. If some roots have grown together, use that to your advantage by keeping them as one unit. When you need a smaller piece, gently give them a tug to pull them apart.

2. Line the basket following the instructions on page 28.

3. You should now have a hole in the center with all the moss roots facing inward. Add a thin layer of potting mix to the bottom of the basket.

4. Set the fuchsia in the center of the basket so that the crown of the plant is even with the top of the basket. Fill in around it with soil so that the ferns will sit at the same level.

5. On opposite corners, squeeze the ferns between the moss roots and the fuchsia. Angle the fern so the fronds spill out over the edges. Fill the gaps with soil.

6. Gently bring the chain and hanger back to the center, adjusting leaves and branches so that the chain can hang properly without pinning back the plants. Water in the plants. Also be sure to water the moss—my preferred method is using a hose, which can easily spray the sides of the basket.

RECIPE 43

CONTEMPORARY GLAZED CERAMIC

cyclamen

*variegated
creeping Charlie*

CONTEMPORARY GLAZED CERAMIC

SEASONS: Fall through spring
LIGHT: Full sun
WATER: High

PLANTS

Three 2-inch (5 cm) red and pink cyclamens (*Cyclamen persicum*)

Three 2-inch (5 cm) variegated creeping Charlies (*Glechoma hederacea* 'Variegata')

CONTAINER & MATERIALS

6-inch-diameter (15 cm) glazed ceramic hanging planter

Potting mix

This small but mighty arrangement, with a vibrant gradient of fuchsia to red cyclamen blooms, is the perfect complement to this pink Half Light Honey planter. The variegated creeping Charlie is easy to grow and prune when it gets too long. Hang this container outside in the mild weather of fall and spring; bring it indoors to enjoy when the weather gets frosty. Cyclamens grow and bloom fall through early spring and go dormant in late spring and summer. Many people treat them as an annual because they are easy to find seasonally; however, you can store the bulbs in a cool, dry place over summer and bring them back out to start their growth cycle again in fall.

1. Fill the bottom half of the planter with potting mix. Place the three cyclamens in a triangle with their flowers tilted slightly outward.

2. Plant the variegated creeping Charlies in the spaces between the cyclamens. Fill the gaps with soil and water in the plants.

SEASONS: Spring through fall
LIGHT: Partial shade
WATER: Moderate

———————

PLANTS

One 4-inch (10 cm) 'Aquamarine' pilea (*Pilea glauca*)

One 4-inch (10 cm) Japanese painted fern (*Athyrium niponicum* 'Pictum')

One 4-inch (10 cm) 'White Wonder' caladium (*Caladium hortulanum*)

One 4-inch (10 cm) silver lace fern (*Pteris ensiformis* 'Evergemiensis')

CONTAINER & MATERIALS

Sphagnum moss

8-inch-diameter (20 cm) Victorian-inspired aged metal hanging basket

Potting mix

1 Soak the moss in water for a few minutes until it is soft, then wring out the excess moisture. Line the hanging basket with at least 2 inches (5 cm) of moss following the instructions on page 28. Add potting mix to fill the bottom half of the basket. Place the pilea on the front right side of the basket, trailing over the rim.

2 Add the Japanese painted fern next to the pilea. These plants have a shorter growth habit, so should be placed at the front of the basket.

3 Plant the caladium at the back right of the basket. Tuck the silver lace fern behind the Japanese painted fern, adding height to the arrangement. Fill the gaps with soil and add a bit more sphagnum moss around the top of the plants to help hold the soil in place. Water in the plants.

METAL ORB

SEASONS: All
LIGHT: Full sun to partial sun
WATER: High

PLANTS

Twenty 2-inch (5 cm) Scotch moss (*Arenaria verna* 'Aurea')

Two 4-inch (10 cm) Scopia 'Gulliver Blue' bacopas (*Chaenostoma cordatum*)

Two 4-inch (10 cm) Penny 'Purple Picotee' violas (*Viola cornuta*)

CONTAINER & MATERIALS

14-inch-diameter (36 cm) metal orb planter

Potting mix

Bacopa is a favorite trailing plant for its cute little flowers that continually bloom. Here the purple variety of bacopa complements low-growing violas that stay neatly contained. Deadhead the violas often to keep them blooming. The bacopas can be pruned back a few inches if they get a bit unruly to encourage new growth.

1. Line a metal orb planter with Scotch moss following the instructions on page 28. Add a handful of potting mix on top of the roots.

2. Plant the the two bacopas on top of the roots of the Scotch moss, one on the left and one on the right.

3. Place the two violas in the middle, filling out the front and back of the planter. Fill the gaps with soil and water in the plants.

Pansy and Viola

PLANT TYPE: Perennials, but often treated as annuals

SEASONS: Fall through spring

LIGHT: Full sun

WATER: High

AVAILABLE COLORS: Yellow, orange, white, pink, blue, purple, red, multicolor

Pansies and violas (both in the *Viola* genus) may seem old-fashioned, but their cheerful flowers never get old. These cool-weather plants provide much-needed color in container gardens when other plants aren't in bloom.

Violas are smaller and more profuse bloomers, with two petals pointing upward and three pointing down, while pansies have three petals pointing upward and one pointing down. Another way to distinguish these plants is by distinct markings: pansies have darker centers or "faces," and violas have black lines that radiate from the center and look like whiskers.

Both plants are compact and easily tucked into any container garden design. They will keep on flowering until the weather warms up if deadheaded regularly. In summer, move your container to shade to extend the bloom time. Many gardeners treat violas and pansies as annuals, because in hot weather the plant will die back and go dormant, but when cool weather returns, the plants will reappear. If flowers are left to go to seed, you're likely to find some friendly volunteers in neighboring pots or beds. Violas and pansies make lovely cut flowers for small flower arrangements. They are also edible, with a mild flavor, making gorgeous bright-colored toppers for cakes, tarts, and salads.

SEASONS: Spring through fall
LIGHT: Partial sun to partial shade
WATER: High

———————

PLANTS

One 1-gallon (4 L) queen's
tears (*Billbergia nutans*)

One 6-inch (15 cm) northern maidenhair
fern (*Adiantum pedatum*)

One 4-inch (10 cm) 'Chinese Butterfly'
ground orchid (*Bletilla ochracea*)

One 4-inch (10 cm) oxalis (*Oxalis triangularis*)

CONTAINER & MATERIALS

14-inch-diameter (36 cm) copper
metal hanging basket

Potting mix

1 Place potting mix in the bottom of the
container. Plant the queen's tears at an
angle so that its leaves arch to one side.
Add more soil to hold it in place.

2 Place the maidenhair fern opposite the
queen's tears, using more soil to hold it in
place. You will have a slight mound of soil in
the middle of the container, sloping down
to the edges.

3 Add the orchid to the front of the container,
angled so that its leaves spill out the front.
Fit the oxalis into the remaining hole. Fill
the gaps with soil and water in the plants.

MODERN COPPER

MODERN CERAMIC

SEASONS: Spring through fall
LIGHT: Partial shade
WATER: Moderate

PLANTS

One 6-inch (15 cm) zig zag
cactus (*Disocactus anguliger*)

One 4-inch (10 cm) 'Santa Cruz'
Sunset begonia (*Begonia boliviensis*)

CONTAINER & MATERIALS

9-inch-diameter (23 cm) white
glazed ceramic planter

Green leather plant hanger

Potting mix

Succulent and cactus potting mix

Black decorative pebbles

This spectacular begonia, with its pendulous vermillion blooms, will flower from spring through the first frost. Pair it with the only foliage that can stand up to its drama: the fabulous zig zag cactus. These plants love a little morning sun but prefer shade in the afternoon.

1. Fill the container halfway with soil, using equal parts standard potting mix and succulent and cactus mix. Combining the two will ensure good drainage, which both plants appreciate.

2. Place the zig zag cactus on the right side of the container. Add more of the combined soils so the begonia will sit at the same height.

3. Plant the begonia on the left side of the container. Fill in around the plants with the mixed soils.

4. Top the container with a layer of decorative pebbles for a clean, polished look. Water in the plants.

CONICAL WICKER

'Siskiyou Blue' fescue

'Rustic Orange' coleus

Greenlee moor grass

CONICAL WICKER

SEASON: Fall

LIGHT: Full sun

WATER: High

PLANTS

One 4-inch (10 cm) 'Rustic Orange' coleus (*Plectranthus scutellarioides*)

One 2-inch (5 cm) Greenlee moor grass (*Sesleria* 'Greenlee Hybrid')

One 2-inch (5 cm) 'Siskiyou Blue' fescue (*Festuca idahoensis*)

CONTAINER & MATERIALS

10-inch-diameter (25 cm) conical wicker hanging basket

Potting mix

This foliage-forward arrangement boasts flowering grasses that signal late summer and fall weather. This warm color palette of burnt oranges and yellows paired with a cone-shaped wicker planter recalls a cornucopia of autumn's bounty.

1. Fill the basket halfway with potting mix. Place the coleus at the front of the container. Add 2 inches (5 cm) more soil. Place the moor grass at the back left side of the container.

2. Add the fescue in the remaining space at the right edge of the container. Fill the gaps with soil and water in the plants.

6

UNCONVENTIONAL CONTAINERS

Almost anything can be turned into a container! This chapter takes things found in nature (like a pumpkin and a log) as well as gardening objects (like a soil sieve and a toolbox) and transforms them into fun and unusual containers. Some objects, like a crate, may already have drain holes; others may need holes drilled into them. Look around your home and see what unexpected items could be turned into planters.

HOLLOW LOG

SEASONS: Spring through fall
LIGHT: Shade
WATER: High

PLANTS

Three 4-inch (10 cm) 'Sunset Velvet' oxalis (*Oxalis spiralis* subsp. *vulcanicola*)

Two 4-inch (10 cm) northern maidenhair ferns (*Adiantum pedatum*)

Two 4-inch (10 cm) bird's-nest ferns (*Asplenium nidus*)

Two 4-inch (10 cm) 'Pink Allusion' arrowhead plants (*Syngonium podophyllum*)

Two 4-inch (10 cm) baby's tears (*Soleirolia soleirolii*)

Six 2-inch (5 cm) Irish moss (*Sagina subulata*)

CONTAINER & MATERIALS

48-inch-long (12 m) hollowed-out log

Potting mix

A hollowed-out log lends itself to creating an arrangement that mimics nature. One trick to achieve this look is spacing the plants irregularly, which creates a more natural, less rigid feeling. *Et voilà!* You've got a log that looks like something you came upon as you were hiking in the woods.

1. Place a thin layer of soil in the bottom of the hollowed-out log. Set the three oxalis across the log, leaving different-size gaps between the plants.

2. Add the maidenhair and bird's-nest ferns, spacing them irregularly across the log. Shift the angles at which you plant them, too, so that some are tilted toward you and others are leaning left or right.

3. Add the arrowhead plants. Here I have picked two plants where one is larger than the other. Variations in size will also naturalize the planting.

4. Nestle the baby's tears and Irish moss between the other plants, placing some of each alongside the log edge so they will trail and spread down the log. Again, leave some patches of bare soil to contrast with areas of dense foliage. Water in the plants.

Oxalis

With cute three- and four-leaf clover-like leaves, oxalis comes in many varieties that perform excellently in container gardens. Also referred to as wood sorrels or shamrocks (in the genus *Oxalis*), these tender perennials (a name for a perennial that's not winter hardy) are often treated as annuals. When the plants go dormant (in summer for some varieties, winter for others), the foliage often dies back, but the plant is still alive under the soil. Oxalis grows from bulbs or rhizomes, so when the plant goes dormant, stop watering and store the plant in a cool, dark, dry place for one to three months, then bring it back into the light and resume watering. You should soon see new growth.

Oxalis are vigorous growers, and you will be charmed by their abundant flowers, which bloom for weeks or months at a time. Depending on the variety, the flowers range from pale purples, strong yellows, and hot pinks to red and white swirls (and bloom in different seasons). Some varieties are perfect for trailing down hanging baskets; others grow upright in clumps. Both forms make excellent fillers and spillers because their shorter stature can hide bare soil and cover stems of leggy plants. With hundreds of varieties, there is an oxalis for any location, full sun to partial shade. They need well-draining soil and moderate water. The hardest part is picking which lucky clover you want to use!

PLANT TYPE: Tender perennial, often treated as an annual

SEASONS: Spring through fall

LIGHT: Full sun to partial shade

WATER: Moderate

AVAILABLE COLORS: Lime green, green, burgundy, purple, gold, pink variegated

GARD-N-TOTE
TOOLBOX

SEASONS: Spring through fall
LIGHT: Full sun
WATER: Moderate

PLANTS

Three 4-inch (10 cm) Easy Breezy Pink sweet alyssums (*Lobularia maritima* 'Balbeezink')

Two 4-inch (10 cm) Namid Early Yellow beggar-ticks (*Bidens ferulifolia* 'KLEBF11764')

Two 3-inch (8 cm) lime mints (*Mentha × piperita* f. *citrata* 'Lime')

Two 2-inch (5 cm) Bonanza Yellow French marigolds (*Tagetes patula* 'PAS2276')

Two 4-inch (10 cm) FlowerPower Spider Purple African daisies (*Osteospermum ecklonis* 'KLEOE16297')

CONTAINER & MATERIALS

18-inch-long (46 cm) vintage yellow metal toolbox

Potting mix

1 Drill six ¼-inch (6 mm) holes in the bottom of the toolbox for drainage. Add a 2-inch (5 cm) layer of potting mix and place the sweet alyssums along the front edge of the box with the flowers spilling out.

2 Place the two yellow beggar-ticks between the sweet alyssums.

3 Add a handful of soil directly behind the middle sweet alyssum so the lime mints and marigolds will sit at the same height as the larger plants. Plant the two lime mints next to each other in the center, the two marigolds on either side, and the African daisies in the back left and right corners. Water in the plants.

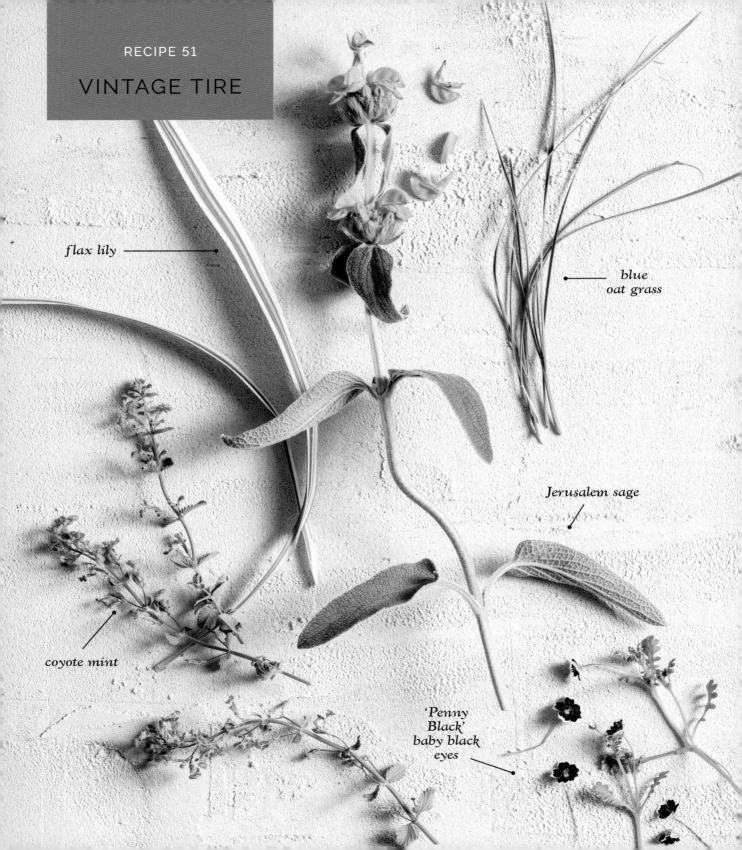

VINTAGE TIRE

flax lily

blue oat grass

Jerusalem sage

coyote mint

'Penny Black' baby black eyes

columbine

Jupiter's beard

VINTAGE TIRE

SEASONS: Spring through fall
LIGHT: Full sun
WATER: Moderate

PLANTS

Two 6-inch (15 cm) flax lilies
(*Dianella tasmanica* 'Variegata')

Two 1-gallon (4 L) Jupiter's beards
(*Centranthus ruber* 'Albus')

Three 4-inch (10 cm) coyote
mints (*Monardella villosa*)

Two 1-gallon (4 L) columbines
(*Aquilegia vulgaris*)

One 3-gallon (11 L) Jerusalem
sage (*Phlomis fruticosa*)

Two 4-inch (10 cm) blue oat grasses
(*Helictotrichon sempervirens*)

Three 4-inch (10 cm) 'Penny
Black' baby black eyes
(*Nemophila menziesii*)

CONTAINER & MATERIALS

Vintage tire (mine was precut
in a rickrack pattern)

Potting mix

Creating a miniature meadow in a large container with densely packed flowering plants is a great way to entice wildlife and pollinator insects to your garden. While many of the plants featured here are drought tolerant, because they are grown in containers they will require more water than usual. Feel free to substitute other pollinator-friendly plants that love full sun and have low water needs. The main idea in this recipe is to pack the tire with as many different flower shapes as possible to attract different types of pollinators. With proper deadheading, many of these flowers will bloom straight through summer.

1. It's best to build this arrangement in its final location because the tire will be quite cumbersome to move. Place 2 to 3 inches (5 to 7.6 cm) of soil in the bottom of the tire.

2. Arrange the largest plants toward the back of the ring (unless the tire will be viewed from all sides, in which case place the largest plants in the center).

3. Add another layer of soil so the medium-size plants will sit at the same depth as the large plants. Arrange the plants in a descending order, with shorter plants in front of taller ones.

4. Add more soil to hold the plants in place. Around the outer edge of the tire, plant the remaining 4-inch (10 cm) plants so that flowers and leaves are spilling over the sides, showcasing the flowers' opulence. Fill the gaps with soil and water in the plants.

BRONZE BUCKET

SEASON: Spring
LIGHT: Full sun
WATER: Moderate

PLANTS

One 6-inch (15 cm) 'Violet
Beauty' tulip (*Tulipa*)

Three 4-inch (10 cm) EverColor
Everlime Japanese sedge
(*Carex oshimensis*)

CONTAINER & MATERIALS

10-inch-diameter (25 cm) antique
bucket, holes drilled if no drainage

Potting mix

Tulips put on a dramatic show when they bloom, quickly changing from tightly closed buds to large, open flowers with arching stems. Grow your tulips from bulbs to witness their entire transformation (see page 26 for a tutorial) or look for plants with lots of tightly closed buds at your local nursery. Here the sedge naturalizes the look of the tulips, making it appear as though a clump popped up through a patch of tall grass and landed in this decorative Turkish bucket.

1. Fill the container halfway with potting mix. Gently place the tulip in the center of the pot. Add a layer of soil to hold it in place.

2. Add the three sedges around half of the container, creating a frame.

3. Fill the gaps with soil and water in the plants.

ANTIQUE WATERING TROUGH

SEASONS: Spring through fall
LIGHT: Partial sun to partial shade
WATER: High

PLANTS

One 4-inch (10 cm) strawberry begonia (*Saxifraga stolonifera*)

One 4-inch (10 cm) sea thrift (*Armeria maritima*)

One 4-inch (10 cm) corkscrew rush (*Juncus effusus 'Spiralis'*)

Twenty 2-inch (5 cm) Scotch moss (*Arenaria verna* 'Aurea')

CONTAINERS & MATERIALS

14-inch-long (36 cm) concrete watering trough

Potting mix

This arrangement is a rare exception where the vessel's lack of drain holes works in our favor because these plants prefer moist soil, and the trough is shallow enough that it will dry out quickly without causing root rot. With a bit of imagination, this asymmetrical arrangement is like a miniature landscape: a forest on one side (where the taller plants are grouped) set against a large meadow (the low-growing Scotch moss, with tiny star-shaped white blooms in late spring). The spiraled leaves of the corkscrew rush mix with the slender flower spikes of the strawberry begonia and sea thrift to add pops of color and tiny flowers that dance above the planting.

1. Add a 1-inch (2.5 cm) layer of soil to the trough. Arrange the begonia, sea thrift, and rush in a group at the left side of the trough.

2. Fill in the rest of the container with the Scotch moss, fitting the plants closely together. Fill the gaps with soil and water in the plants.

Scotch Moss and Irish Moss

PLANT TYPE: Evergreen perennial

SEASONS: Spring through fall

LIGHT: Full sun to partial shade

WATER: High

AVAILABLE COLORS: Various shades of green

Often used as a ground cover, Scotch moss (*Arenaria verna*) and Irish moss (*Sagina subulata*) are two of my go-tos for underplanting containers because of their ability to blanket bare soil and provide a lush finish to a design. I also favor them for lining baskets because they add a vibrancy not found with dried moss. And in late spring and summer, you can't help but swoon as these two mosses sprout the most delicate tiny white flowers!

When choosing between the two varieties, consider the palette of your container: Scotch moss is a vibrant, almost lime-green color; Irish moss is a deeper, saturated green hue. The brighter green can create contrast and stand out against other plants, while the darker green tends to blend in and create a nice backdrop for other plants to shine.

Scotch and Irish moss also act as mulch, slowing the evaporation of moisture from container soil. In cooler weather, these mosses grow best in full sun, but in heat they appreciate partial shade. (Unlike true mosses, Scotch and Irish moss will get leggy in full-shade conditions.) Watering moss can be a bit tricky because it doesn't like to dry out, nor does it like soggy soil. To achieve this balance, make sure water drains freely from your container, so you can water deeply without leaving the soil too damp. The best tip is to keep your eyes on it, as it may need watering every day in the heat of summer.

SOIL SIEVE

SEASONS: All
LIGHT: Partial sun
WATER: Low

PLANTS

Six 2-inch (5 cm) coral cacti
(*Rhipsalis cereuscula*)

Five 3-inch (8 cm) 'Ruby Slippers'
echeverias (*Echeveria harmsii*)

Two 2-inch (5 cm) baby's necklaces
(*Crassula rupestris × C. perforata*)

Three 2-inch (5 cm) 'Debbie'
graptoverias (× *Graptoveria*)

Five 2-inch (5 cm) 'Worthy One'
graptoverias (× *Graptoveria*)

Three 2-inch (5 cm) 'Black Knight'
echeverias (*Echeveria affinis*)

Two 1-inch (3 cm) 'Platinum'
graptoverias (× *Graptoveria*)

One 2-inch (5 cm) 'Gray Curl'
echeveria (*Echeveria*)

CONTAINER & MATERIALS

12-inch (30 cm) soil sieve
with a fine-mesh screen and
a wide-mesh screen

12-inch (30 cm) piece jute twine

Succulent and cactus potting mix

Bring some color to a blank wall or door with a succulent wall-hanging arrangement. A few keys to a successful composition: create groupings of the same variety, use repetition, and cluster the plants close together.

Here we are using a soil sieve to hold the plants and soil in place. Soil sieves are often made of metal or wood and have different-gauge mesh liners designed to filter out large soil clumps. For this project, you want two different filters: a fine mesh to keep the soil from washing away and a wide gauge through which we'll make small gaps for planting the succulents.

1. Insert the fine-mesh screen into the back of the sieve. Decide which side is the top and use the jute to tie a hanging loop through the mesh on the back of the sieve.

2. Fill the sieve with potting mix almost to the top edge. Wedge the wide-gauge screen into the top of the sieve.

3. Arrange the succulents off to the side into a planting pattern. Placing the same plant in groups of three or more will provide the basic structure to your design. Other plants can be used as accents, and patterns can be mirrored from top to bottom or left to right as a way to create unity.

4. Start planting from the center of the sieve, working your way to the outside edges. Use wire cutters to cut small holes in the wide screen, then spread the wires apart a bit to make space to insert the plants. The base of each succulent should sit on the screen. Top off each plant with a few pinches of soil and push the wires back around each root-ball to hold it in place.

5. Once your arrangement is planted, fill any gaps with soil and water in the plants. The sieve should hold the plants in place so that the completed sieve can hang vertically on the wall, but if you notice that some plants are loose, wait a few weeks for the roots to take hold in their new home before hanging the arrangement.

COPPER WATER DISPENSER

Sunsatia Cranberry
Red nemesia

basil

'Elan' strawberry

COPPER WATER DISPENSER

SEASONS: Spring through fall
LIGHT: Full sun
WATER: High

PLANTS

One 6-inch (15 cm) basil
(*Ocimum basilicum*)

Two 4-inch (10 cm) Sunsatia
Cranberry Red nemesias
(*Nemesia* 'Innemcrare')

Three 4-inch (10 cm) 'Elan'
strawberries (*Fragaria × ananassa*)

CONTAINER & MATERIALS

14-inch (36 cm) antique
copper water dispenser

Potting mix

Strawberries and basil are a delicious culinary combination as well as happy companions in the garden. The abundant flowers of the red nemesia attract pollinators, which will help strawberry plants produce more fruit, and the strong scent of the basil will deter pests from eating the berries before you do!

1. The water dispenser has a spigot where water can run out, but drill a few extra holes in the center of the container to ensure good drainage. Fill the container three-quarters of the way with potting mix. Place the basil at the back center of the copper dispenser.

2. Add 3 inches (7.6 cm) of soil. Place the nemesias on either side of the basil, toward the left and right edges of the container.

3. Evenly space the three strawberry plants across the front of the container so the flowers and fruits are positioned to trail down the sides. Fill the gaps with soil and water in the plants.

BLUE MILK
CRATE

SEASONS: Spring through fall
LIGHT: Full to partial sun
WATER: High

———

PLANTS

Two 4-inch (10 cm) Superbells White calibrachoas (*Calibrachoa × hybrida*)

One 4-inch (10 cm) 'Tangerine Gem' signet marigold (*Tagetes tenufolia*)

One 6-inch (15 cm) Elanos 'Pastel Orange' geranium (*Pelargonium × hortorum*)

Two 4-inch (10 cm) Under the Sea 'Barracuda' coleus (*Plectranthus scutellarioides*)

CONTAINER & MATERIALS

13-inch (33 cm) blue milk crate

Forest moss

Potting mix

1 Line the container bottom and all the way up the sides with forest moss. As you work, add potting mix to hold the moss in place. Continue until the moss reaches the top of the crate. Place the calibrachoas on the front corner and right side of the crate, so that the leaves and flowers spill over the edge.

2 Plant the marigold in the back corner of the crate.

3 Set the geranium in the center of the crate. Plant the coleus in the right and left corners. Fill the gaps with soil and water in the plants.

SEASON: Fall
LIGHT: Full to partial sun
WATER: Moderate

———————

PLANTS

One 4-inch (10 cm) 'Staviski Orange' Belgian mum (*Chrysanthemum × morifolium*)

One 4-inch (10 cm) FlameThrower Habanero coleus (*Plectranthus scutellarioides* 'UF09-8-37')

One 4-inch (10 cm) bush morning glory (*Convolvulus cneorum*)

One 4-inch (10 cm) purple fountain grass (*Pennisetum setaceum* 'Rubrum')

CONTAINER & MATERIALS

14-inch (36 cm) pumpkin

Petroleum jelly or paraffin wax (optional)

8-inch (20 cm) plastic pot and saucer

Potting mix

Forest moss

1 Carve a 10-inch (25 cm) hole at the top of the pumpkin. Scoop out the seeds and fibers, so the interior is as clean and dry as possible. To extend the life of the planting, you can apply a thin layer of petroleum jelly or paraffin to the inside of the pumpkin. Place the plastic pot and saucer inside the pumpkin, and fill the pot three-quarters of the way with potting mix. Set the mum on the left side of the pot.

2 Insert the coleus at the right side of the arrangement.

3 Plant the bush morning glory at the front of the pot. Insert the grass at the back. Fill the gaps with soil and water in the plants. Top off the arrangement with pieces of forest moss. The pumpkin should last for about a month; the plastic planter can then be lifted out and potted in another container, or the plants transferred to the garden.

RESOURCES

BUYING PLANTS

When shopping for plants and pots, I encourage you to first go to your locally owned nurseries over big-box stores. Not only will you be supporting your community, but you'll find quality, seasonal plants and passionate plant people who will be able to field all your questions. Here is a collection of my favorite Bay Area spots for plants and planters.

Ace Garden Center
4001 Grand Avenue, Oakland, CA 94610

Berkeley Horticultural Nursery
1310 McGee Avenue, Berkeley, CA 94703

The Dry Garden Nursery
6556 Shattuck Avenue, Oakland, CA 94609

Flora Grubb Gardens
1634 Jerrold Avenue, San Francisco, CA 94124

Flowerland
330 Solano Avenue, Albany, CA 94706

INFORMATION ON PESTS & DISEASES

Attracting Beneficial Bugs to Your Garden: A Natural Approach to Pest Control by Jessica Walliser

An excellent guide to help you select, care for, and place plants that will attract beneficial insects for natural pest control.

Gardeningknowhow.com

Visit their "Problems" page for pest and disease profiles along with tips for dealing with weather and environmental stressors and weeds.

Missouribotanicalgarden.org

Visit their "Help for the Home Gardener" page for in-depth guides to identifying and preventing pests and diseases, as well as strategies to treat and control them.

The Organic Gardener's Handbook of Natural Insect and Disease Control edited by Barbara W. Ellis and Fern Marshall Bradley

An easy-to-use encyclopedia-style book with images to identify pests, beneficial insects, and diseases. It provides preventive ideas and organic solutions to pests and diseases in the garden.

INFORMATION ON VEGETABLE GARDENING

Field Guide to Urban Gardening: How to Grow Plants, No Matter Where You Live by Kevin Espiritu

A great resource with tons of strategies for gardening in small spaces, from vertical gardens to balconies.

The First-Time Gardener: Growing Vegetables by Jessica Sowards

An in-depth guide to designing and creating a vegetable garden.

Small-Space Vegetable Gardens: Growing Great Edibles in Containers, Raised Beds, and Small Plots by Andrea Bellamy

An in-depth resource for vegetable gardening in containers year-round.

The Year-Round Vegetable Gardener by Niki Jabbour

A handbook for growing successful vegetable gardens in any climate.

INFORMATION ON COMPANION PLANTING

Great Garden Companions: A Companion-Planting System for a Beautiful, Chemical-Free Vegetable Garden by Sally Jean Cunningham

A comprehensive gardening guide focusing on vegetable, flower, and herb combinations for an organic approach to minimizing pests and diseases.

Natural Companions: The Garden Lover's Guide to Plant Combinations by Ken Druse

A seasonal guide to pairing plants that complement one another and bloom at the same time.

Perennial Combinations: Stunning Combinations That Make Your Garden Look Fantastic Right from the Start by C. Colston Burrell

A great design resource for the garden that can be applied to a single container or groupings of containers.

Plant Partners: Science-Based Companion Planting Strategies for the Vegetable Garden by Jessica Walliser

A research-backed guide to plant combinations that will help improve soil, deter pests, and increase biodiversity in the garden.

PLANT INDEX

Following is a more detailed look at the plants called for in the preceding recipes. Use this as a guide to determine which plants are appropriate for your specific growing conditions (hardiness zone, light conditions, etc.) and mix and match plants to design your own container garden creations!

BOTANICAL NAME	COMMON NAME(S)	PLANT TYPE	HARDINESS ZONES	GROWTH HABIT	COLORS	BLOOM TIME	SUN	WATER	FEATURED ON PAGE(S)
Acer palmatum var. *dissectum* 'Tamukeyama'	'Tamukeyama' lacy Japanese maple	deciduous perennial	5 to 8	tree	burgundy	spring	full sun to part shade	moderate	45
Adiantum hispidulum	rosy maidenhair fern	semi-evergreen	9 to 11	mounding	amber and green	n/a	part shade to shade	high	34
Adiantum pedatum	northern maidenhair fern	deciduous perennial	3 to 8	upright	green	n/a	part sun to shade	high	174, 184
Aeonium arboreum 'Zwartkop'	'Zwartkop' black rose aeonium	monocarpic	9 to 12	upright	yellow flowers	summer	full sun to part sun	low	102
Agastache	hummingbird mint	herbaceous perennial	5 to 10	upright	orange, pink, red	summer and fall	full sun	moderate	94
Alocasia 'Regal Shields'	'Regal Shields' elephant ear	perennial	9 to 11	upright	white	spring and summer	part sun to shade	high	120
Aloe vera	aloe vera	perennial	9 to 11	upright	yellow	fall	full sun to part sun	low	75
Anigozanthos flavidus	kangaroo paw	evergreen	10 to 11	upright	yellow, orange, red, pink, purple	spring to fall	full sun to part shade	moderate	97
Aquilegia	columbine	flowering perennial	3 to 8	mounding	blue, violet, white, pink, red	April and May	full sun to part shade	moderate	115, 192
Arenaria verna 'Aurea'	Scotch moss	evergreen, herbaceous perennial	4 to 8	spreading	white	spring	full sun to part sun	moderate to high	149, 170, 196, 198
Armeria maritima	sea thrift	evergreen	3 to 9	upright mounding	pink, lavender, white	spring and summer	full sun to part shade	moderate	196
Asparagus densiflorus	asparagus fern	evergreen perennial	11 to 12	mounding	green; pinkish white flowers	spring to fall	sun to part shade	moderate	60, 76
Asplenium nidus	bird's-nest fern	evergreen perennial	9 to 11	mounding rosette	green	n/a	part shade to shade	moderate	184
Athyrium niponicum 'Pictum'	Japanese painted fern	perennial	5 to 8	upright	gray-green	n/a	part shade to shade	moderate	169
Begonia × argenteo guttata	angel wing begonia	flowering perennial	10 to 11	upright	red, pink, white, orange	spring to fall	part shade to shade	high	34

BOTANICAL NAME	COMMON NAME(S)	PLANT TYPE	HARDINESS ZONES	GROWTH HABIT	COLORS	BLOOM TIME	SUN	WATER	FEATURED ON PAGE(S)
Begonia boliviensis 'Santa Cruz'	Bolivian begonia	deciduous perennial	7 to 10	upright	vermillion	spring until frost	part sun	moderate	176
Begonia 'Tiger Paws'	'Tiger Paws' rhizomatous begonia	evergreen	10 to 11	creeping	pink and white	late winter and spring	part shade	medium	140
Begonia × tuberosa	tuberous begonia	perennial tuber	10 to 11	upright	white, yellow, pink, coral, orange, red	summer and fall	part sun	moderate to high	149
Bidens ferulifolia	beggar-ticks	annual, perennial	8 to 11	upright	yellow, white, pink, orange	summer	full sun	moderate	52, 189
Billbergia nutans	queen's tears	perennial	10 to 11	upright, fountain	pink, purple, yellow, green, red	spring to fall	part shade	moderate	174
Blechnum gibbum	silver lady fern, dwarf tree fern	perennial	11 to 12	upright	green	n/a	part shade to shade	high	109
Bletilla ochracea 'Chinese Butterfly'	'Chinese Butterfly' ground orchid	perennial	6 to 10	upright	yellow	spring and summer	part sun	moderate	174
Brassica oleracea	ornamental kale	biennial, treated as annual	7 to 10	rosette	pink, purple, red, white leaves	fall, winter, spring	full sun to part sun	moderate to high	78, 132
Caladium hortulanum	caladium	perennial, treated as annual	9 to 11	upright	green, white, pink, red, multicolored	spring to fall	part sun to shade	moderate	109
Calendula officinalis	pot marigold	perennial, treated as annual	2 to 11	upright	yellow, orange, white, apricot	late spring to fall	full sun	moderate	102
Calibrachoa × hybrida	million bells	perennial, treated as annual	3 to 11	sprawling	violet, blue, pink, red, yellow, white	summer	full sun to part sun	high	156, 161, 207
Canna 'Red King Humbert'	canna lily	perennial bulb	8 to 11	upright	reddish orange	summer and fall	full sun	moderate	76
Carex buchananii	leatherleaf sedge	evergreen	6 to 9	upright	brown	summer	full sun to part shade	moderate to high	128
Carex oshimensis	Japanese sedge	evergreen	6 to 9	upright	brown	spring	full sun to part sun	moderate to high	195
Catharanthus roseus 'Cora Cascade Violet'	'Cora Cascade Violet' vinca	annual	9 to 11	trailing	purple, pink	spring until frost	full sun to part shade	moderate	54
Centranthus ruber 'Albus'	'Albus' Jupiter's beard	herbaceous perennial	5 to 8	upright	white, pink	spring and early summer	full sun to part shade	moderate	192
Cephalocereus senilis	old man cactus	cactus	9 to 10	columnar	pink, red, yellow, white	spring	full sun to part sun	low	152
Chaenostoma cordatum	bacopa	herbaceous perennial, treated as annual	9 to 11	trailing	white, lavender, purple	late spring through fall	full sun to part sun	high	170

BOTANICAL NAME	COMMON NAME(S)	PLANT TYPE	HARDINESS ZONES	GROWTH HABIT	COLORS	BLOOM TIME	SUN	WATER	FEATURED ON PAGE(S)
Chrysanthemum × morifolium	Belgian mum	perennial	5 to 9	mounding	white, yellow, pink, orange, red, bicolor	late summer and fall	full sun	high	208
Colocasia esculenta	taro	perennial	9 to 11	upright	green, white spathe	spring to fall	part sun to shade	high	120
Convolvulus cneorum	bush morning glory, silver bush	perennial	8 to 10	upright	white	spring and summer	full sun	moderate to low	208
Cordyline fruticosa	ti plant	perennial	9 to 11	upright	white	summer	full sun	moderate to high	47, 123
Coreopsis	tickseed	perennial or annual	4 to 10	upright	yellow, orange, rose, lavender, white, bicolor	summer and fall	full sun to part shade	moderate to low	71, 78
Cosmos bipinnatus	cosmos	perennial, treated as annual	9 to 11	upright	pink, orange, red, yellow, white, bicolor	summer until frost	full sun	moderate	94
Craspedia globosa	sun balls	tender perennial, treated as annual	8 to 11	upright	yellow	summer until frost	full sun	moderate to low	150
Crassula rupestris × C. perforata	baby's necklace	succulent	9 to 11	branching	pale pink	spring	full sun to part sun	low	201
Cuphea ramosissima	cuphea	annual	10 to 11	mounding	pink	spring until frost	full sun to part sun	moderate	88
Cupressus sempervirens	Italian cypress	evergreen	7 to 10	upright	green	spring	full sun	moderate to low	105
Cyclamen persicum	cyclamen	herbaceous perennial	9 to 11	mounding	white, pinks, lavender, red	winter and spring	full sun to part shade	moderate	63, 105, 166
Cyperus alternifolius	umbrella papyrus	perennial	9 to 12	upright	yellow-green	late summer and early fall	full sun to part shade	high	120
Cyperus isocladus	dwarf papyrus	perennial, treated as annual	9 to 12	upright	yellow-green	late summer and early fall	full sun to part shade	high	146
Dianella tasmanica	flax lily	evergreen	9 to 11	upright	blue	spring	full sun to part shade	moderate to low	192
Dianthus caryophyllus	carnation	herbaceous perennial, treated as annual	7 to 10	upright	pinks, reds, whites, lavender, yellow, orange, bicolor	late spring and summer	full sun	moderate	83
Diascia	twinspur	perennial, treated as annual	5 to 9	upright	pink, white, orange, red	spring and fall	full sun to part sun	moderate to low	83
Digitalis purpurea	foxglove	biennial	4 to 9	upright	red, pink, yellow, white, purple	early summer	full sun to part sun	high	112
Disocactus anguliger	zig zag cactus	evergreen	10 and 11	trailing	white, pale yellow	late summer and fall	part sun to shade	moderate to low	176

BOTANICAL NAME	COMMON NAME(S)	PLANT TYPE	HARDINESS ZONES	GROWTH HABIT	COLORS	BLOOM TIME	SUN	WATER	FEATURED ON PAGE(S)
Dryopteris erythrosora	autumn fern	evergreen, herbaceous perennial	5 to 9	upright	reddish green	n/a	part sun to shade	high	149
Dymondia margaretae	silver carpet	perennial	9 to 11	ground cover	yellow	spring to fall	full sun to part sun	moderate	150
Echeveria 'Gray Curl'	'Gray Curl' echeveria	succulent	9 to 11	rosette	orange, yellow	spring	full sun to shade	moderate	201
Echeveria affinis 'Black Knight'	'Black Knight' echeveria	succulent	10	rosette	red	fall and winter	full sun to part sun	moderate	201
Echeveria 'Crinoline Ruffles'	'Crinoline Ruffles' echeveria	succulent	9 to 11	rosette	pink	late summer	full sun to shade	moderate	118
Echeveria harmsii 'Ruby Slippers'	'Ruby Slippers' echeveria	succulent	10 to 11	shrub	orange	late winter, late summer	full sun to part shade	moderate	75, 201
Echinacea	coneflower	herbaceous perennial	3 to 9	upright	white, yellow, pink, orange, purple, green, red	summer and fall	full sun	moderate	51
Echinacea purpurea	purple coneflower	herbaceous perennial	3 to 8	upright	purplish pink	summer and fall	full sun to part shade	moderate	94
Erigeron karvinskainus	Latin American fleabane	perennial	4 to 9	spreading mat	white, pink, yellow, purple, blue	mid-summer to fall	full sun to part sun	moderate	97
Euphorbia amygdaloides	spurge	herbaceous perennial	6 to 8	upright	yellow	spring and early summer	full sun to part shade	low	97
Euphorbia leucadendron	cat tails euphorbia	succulent	9 to 11	upright	yellow green	spring and summer	full sun	low	143
Euphorbia trigona 'Rubra'	'Rubra' African milk tree	succulent	8 to 12	upright	white, yellow	spring and summer	full sun to part sun	low	48
Farfugium japonicum	leopard plant	perennial	7 to 10	clumping	yellow	fall	part shade to shade	high	140
Festuca idahoensis 'Siskiyou Blue'	Idaho blue fescue	perennial	4 to 8	mounding	yellow, cream	summer	full sun to part shade	moderate to low	88, 143, 180
Fragaria × ananassa	strawberry	perennial evergreen	4 to 8	rosette	white	May and June flowers, July and August fruit	full sun to part shade	high	204
Fuchsia 'Seventh Heaven'	'Seventh Heaven' giant fuchsia	deciduous perennial	8 to 11	trailing	White and pink	summer and fall	part sun to shade	high	162
Gazania rigens	treasure flower	tender perennial, treated as annual	9 to 11	clumping, trailing	yellow, orange, pink, white	late spring and summer	full sun	moderate	88, 150
Glechoma hederacea	creeping Charlie	perennial, treated as annual	5 to 10	trailing	purple, pink	spring	full sun to shade	moderate	166

BOTANICAL NAME	COMMON NAME(S)	PLANT TYPE	HARDINESS ZONES	GROWTH HABIT	COLORS	BLOOM TIME	SUN	WATER	FEATURED ON PAGE(S)
× *Graptoveria*	graptoveria	succulent	9	rosette	purple, pink	spring and summer	part sun	low	201
Hedera helix	English ivy	evergreen	4 to 8	trailing, spreading	yellow-green	fall	full sun to shade	moderate	115
Helichrysum petiolare	licorice plant	tender perennial, treated as annual	9 to 10	trailing, spreading	white	summer	full sun to part shade	moderate	54, 57, 76
Helictotrichon sempervirens	blue oat grass	perennial grass	4 to 8	mounding	blue-brown	summer	full sun	low	192
Helleborus argutifolius	hellebore	herbaceous perennial	3 to 9	upright	white, pink, green, maroon, purple	late winter and spring	part sun to shade	moderate	83, 84
Heuchera	coralbells	herbaceous perennial	4 to 9	mounding	green, yellow, reds, orange, purples, silver, multicolored foliage	late spring and summer	full sun to shade	moderate to high	34, 47, 65, 112, 138, 156
× *Heucherella*	foamy bells	herbaceous perennial	4 to 9	mounding	chartreuse, coral, amber, purples, reds, oranges, multicolored foliage	spring and summer	full sun to shade	moderate to high	136
Hydrangea macrophylla	bigleaf hydrangea	perennial	3 to 9	upright	blue, white, pink, green, red	spring to fall	part sun to part shade	moderate to high	65
Hylotelephium 'Blue Pearl'	'Blue Pearl' sedum	succulent, herbaceous perennial	3 to 9	clumping	pink to white	fall	full sun	low	118, 152
Impatiens hawkeri	New Guinea impatiens	herbaceous perennial, treated as annual	10 to 11	mounding	orange	late spring through fall	full sun to part shade	moderate	54
Ipomoea batatas	sweet potato vine	annual, tender perennial	9 to 11	trailing, spreading	green, chartreuse, purple, bicolor	spring and summer	full sun to part sun	moderate	109, 128, 149
Isolepis cernua	fiber-optic grass	tender perennial, treated as annual	8 to 10	clumping	white, brown	summer	full sun	moderate to high	136
Jacobaea maritima	dusty miller	tender perennial, treated as annual	7 to 10	mounding	purple	summer	full sun	moderate	63, 105
Juncus effusus 'Spiralis'	corkscrew rush	semi-evergreen	4 to 9	upright	cream, tan, white	spring	full sun to part shade	high	196
Kalanchoe fedtschenkoi 'Variegata'	variegated lavender scallop	succulent	9 to 11	upright	pink, mauve	spring and summer	full sun to part sun	low	152
Kalanchoe tomentosa	panda plant	succulent	11 to 12	mounding	green, yellow	summer	full sun to part sun	low	152

BOTANICAL NAME	COMMON NAME(S)	PLANT TYPE	HARDINESS ZONES	GROWTH HABIT	COLORS	BLOOM TIME	SUN	WATER	FEATURED ON PAGE(S)
Lamium	dead nettle, spotted dead nettle	perennial, treated as annual	4 to 8	spreading	purple, white, pink	spring and summer	part sun to shade	high	83
Lamium galeobdolon	yellow archangel	herbaceous perennial, treated as annual	4 to 9	trailing, spreading	yellow	spring	part shade to shade	moderate to low	115
Lantana montevidensis	trailing lantana	perennial, treated as annual	10 to 11	upright, trailing	white, yellow, orange, red, pink, purple, multicolored	late spring to fall	full sun	moderate	52
Lemna minor	duckweed	perennial aquatic plant	4 to 10	free floating	green spadix	summer	full sun to part shade	water	98
Leucanthemum vulgare	oxeye daisy	herbaceous perennial	3 to 8	upright	white with yellow center	late spring to mid-summer	full sun to part sun	moderate to low	71
Libertia peregrinans	New Zealand iris	perennial	8 to 10	upright	white	late spring to early summer	full sun to part sun	moderate	102
Lobelia erinus	lobelia	tender perennial, treated as annual	10 to 11	trailing, upright	white, blue, violet, purple, red, pink	spring to fall	full sun to part sun	moderate to high	38, 161
Lobularia maritima	sweet alyssum	annual, tender perennial	5 to 9	trailing, spreading	white, purple, pink, peach	spring and fall	full sun to part sun	moderate to high	189
Lotus berthelotii	parrot's beak	evergreen	10 to 12	trailing, climbing	orange-red	spring to fall	full sun	moderate	156
Lysimachia nummularia	creeping Jenny	herbaceous perennial	3 to 9	trailing	chartreuse, green, gold foliage	summer	full sun to part shade	moderate to high	65, 109
Mentha × piperita f. *citrata* 'Lime'	lime mint	perennial	4 to 9	upright	lime green foliage, purple flowers	summer and fall	full sun	high	189
Miscanthus sinensis 'Strictus'	'Strictus' eulalia	herbaceous perennial	5 to 9	upright, clumping	pink	late summer	full sun to part shade	moderate	71
Monardella villosa	coyote mint	perennial	7 to 10	shrub	pink-lavender	late spring to summer	full sun to part sun	low	192
Muehlenbeckia complexa 'Big Leaf'	'Big Leaf' creeping wire vine	evergreen	7 to 10	climbing, trailing	white	spring	full sun to part sun	high	136
Myriophyllum aquaticum	parrot's feather	perennial	6 to 10	water plant	pinkish white	spring and fall	full sun to part sun	wet	98
Narcissus	daffodil, jonquil, narcissus	perennial bulbs	3 to 9	upright, clumping	yellow, white, peach, bicolor	spring	full sun to part sun	moderate	38, 41
Nassella tenuissima	Mexican feather grass	perennial	7 to 11	clumping	green	summer	full sun	moderate to low	143
Nemesia	nemesia	annual, short-lived perennial	2 to 10	upright, trailing	red, pink, white, purple, blue, bicolor	spring and summer	full sun to part sun	high	204

BOTANICAL NAME	COMMON NAME(S)	PLANT TYPE	HARDINESS ZONES	GROWTH HABIT	COLORS	BLOOM TIME	SUN	WATER	FEATURED ON PAGE(S)
Nemophila menziesii 'Penny Black'	baby black eyes	annual	2 to 11	upright, spreading	blue, white, black, bicolor	late winter to early summer	full sun to part sun	moderate	192
Nephrolepis exaltata	Boston fern	perennial, treated as annual	9 to 11	upright, clumping	green	n/a	part shade to shade	high	120, 161
Ocimum basilicum	sweet basil	annual	2 to 11	upright	white, pink	summer	full sun	high to moderate	204
Ocimum basilicum 'Dark Opal'	'Dark Opal' purple basil	annual	2 to 11	upright	pink	summer	full sun	high to moderate	90
Ocimum minimum	bush basil	perennial, treated as annual	11	bush	purple	summer	full sun	moderate	90
Oenothera speciosa	pink evening primrose	herbaceous perennial	4 to 9	spreading	white to pink	early summer	full sun	moderate	68
Ophiopogon planiscapus 'Nigrescens'	'Nigrescens' black mondo grass	perennial	5 to 9	low mounding	lavender	summer	full sun to part sun	moderate	45, 88
Opuntia microdasys	bunny ears cactus	evergreen perennial	8 to 12	upright	yellow	spring and early summer	full sun to part sun	low	143
Origanum 'Kent Beauty'	ornamental oregano	semi-evergreen	6 to 9	bush	chartreuse to pale pink, purple	summer	full sun	moderate to low	132
Ornithogalum dubium	orange star, star of Bethlehem	perennial bulbs	7 to 11	upright bulb	orange	early winter and spring	full sun	moderate	38
Osteospermum ecklonis	African daisy, Cape daisy	herbaceous perennial, treated as annual	10 to 11	upright	orange, pink, white, purple, yellow, red	spring to fall	full sun	moderate	102, 123, 189
Oxalis	oxalis, false shamrock, wood sorrel	perennial, treated as annual	9 to 10	upright, trailing	pink, yellow, lavender, orange, white	spring, winter, summer, fall	full sun to shade	moderate	63, 140, 174, 184, 187
Papaver nudicaule	Iceland poppy	perennial, treated as annual	2 to 7	upright	yellow, red, pink, champagne, orange, white	late spring and summer	full sun to part sun	moderate to high	52, 156
Pelargonium × hortorum	geranium	evergreen perennial, treated as annual	10 to 11	mounding upright	white, red, pink, purple, mauve, orange, and reddish black	spring to fall	part shade to full sun	moderate to high	76, 207
Pennisetum glaucum	ornamental millet	perennial, treated as annual	10 to 11	upright, clumping	purple, gold	fall	full sun	moderate	78
Pennisetum setaceum 'Rubrum'	purple fountain grass	tender perennial	9 and up	upright, fountain	burgundy, purple	fall	full sun	moderate to low	208

BOTANICAL NAME	COMMON NAME(S)	PLANT TYPE	HARDINESS ZONES	GROWTH HABIT	COLORS	BLOOM TIME	SUN	WATER	FEATURED ON PAGE(S)
Pentas lanceolata	star flower	herbaceous perennial, treated as annual	10 to 11	upright	red, white, pink, lavender	summer and fall	full sun to part sun	moderate	132
Petrosedum sediforme 'Turquoise Tails'	'Turquoise Tails' stonecrop	succulent	5 to 10	ground cover	yellow	early summer	full sun to part sun	low	118
Petunia × atkinsiana	petunia	herbaceous perennial, treated as annual	9 to 11	trailing, spreading	blue, purple, white, red, yellow, orange, pink, multicolored	spring to fall	full sun	moderate to high	68
Petunia × Calibrachoa	petchoa	herbaceous perennial, treated as annual	10 to 11	trailing	red, pink, white, orange, purple, yellow, bicolor	spring to fall	full sun to part sun	moderate to high	128
Phlomis fruticosa	Jerusalem sage	evergreen, perennial	8 to 11	upright, bush	yellow	summer	full sun	moderate to low	192
Pilea glauca 'Aquamarine'	'Aquamarine' red-stemmed pilea	tropical perennial, treated as annual	8 to 11	trailing, ground cover	cream, pink, peach	spring	part shade to shade	moderate to low	169
Pistia stratiotes	water lettuce	perennial evergreen	9 to 11	rosette	greenish yellow to cream	summer	full sun to part sun	water plant	95
Platycodon grandiflorus	balloon flower	perennial	3 to 8	upright	purple	summer	full sun to part sun	moderate	161
Plectranthus scutellarioides	coleus	tender perennial, treated as annual	11	upright	purple, red, orange, pink, green, yellow, multicolored foliage	late summer	part sun to shade	moderate	47, 123, 125, 136, 180, 207, 208
Polystichum munitum	western sword fern	evergreen	5 to 9	clumping	green	n/a	part shade to shade	high	162
Pontederia crassipes	water hyacinth	aquatic perennial, treated as annual	8 to 11	clumping, spreading	purple	summer	full sun to part sun	water plant	98, 101
Portulaca oleracea	purslane	annual	5 to 10	spreading, trailing	yellow, orange, pink, white	spring to late summer	full sun	moderate to low	123
Pteris ensiformis	silver lace fern	evergreen	8 to 10	upright	green and white	n/a	part shade to shade	high	169
Ranunculus asiaticus	Persian buttercup	perennial bulb	8 to 10	clumping, upright	cream, yellow, orange, apricot, pink, red	spring	full sun	moderate	156
Rhipsalis cereuscula	coral cactus	evergreen succulent	10 to 11	shrub	white	year-round	part sun	low to moderate	201
Rosmarinus officinalis	rosemary	evergreen	8 to 11	shrub	blue	winter and spring	full sun	low to moderate	51, 156

BOTANICAL NAME	COMMON NAME(S)	PLANT TYPE	HARDINESS ZONES	GROWTH HABIT	COLORS	BLOOM TIME	SUN	WATER	FEATURED ON PAGE(S)
Rumex sanguineus	red-veined sorrel	perennial, treated as annual	4 to 8	clumping	green to reddish brown	June and July	full sun	moderate	112
Salvia microphylla 'Hot Lips'	'Hot Lips' salvia	perennial	6 to 9	woody shrub	pink, red, white, bicolor	spring through fall	full sun to part sun	moderate to low	54
Salvia officinalis	common sage	herbaceous perennial	4 to 10	upright	blue	June	full sun	moderate to low	51
Saxifraga stolonifera	strawberry begonia	herbaceous perennial	6 to 9	clumping, spreading	white	May and June	full sun to shade	moderate	196
Scleranthus biflorus	Australian astroturf	perennial	9 to 11	ground cover	yellow-green	summer	full sun to part sun	moderate	45
Sedum album subsp. *teretifolium* 'Murale'	'Murale' white stonecrop	succulent	3 to 8	spreading	whitish pink	summer	full sun to part sun	moderate to low	48
Sedum morganianum	burro's tail	evergreen succulent	10 to 11	trailing, spreading	reddish purple	summer	full sun to part sun	low	75
Selaginella kraussiana 'Aurea'	golden spikemoss	evergreen, treated as annual	11 to 12	ground cover	golden green	n/a	part sun to shade	high	146
Senecio radicans	fishhooks	tender perennial, succulent	10	trailing	white	fall and winter	part sun	low	75
Sesleria 'Greenlee Hybrid'	Greenlee moor grass	perennial grass	5 to 9	mounding	silvery, purple, white	spring and summer	full sun to part shade	moderate to low	180
Solanum lycopersicum 'Sungold'	'Sungold' cherry tomato	annual	3 to 11	upright	yellow	summer	full sun	moderate to high	90
Soleirolia soleirolii	baby's tears	evergreen	9 to 11	trailing	creamy white	May and June	part shade to shade	moderate	52, 184
Stachys byzantina	lamb's-ear	herbaceous perennial	4 to 9	clumping	lavender	late spring and early summer	full sun to part shade	moderate	102
Syngonium podophyllum	arrowhead plant	herbaceous perennial, treated as annual	10 and 11	trailing, climbing	greenish white spadix	summer	part sun to shade	moderate to high	184
Tagetes patula	French marigold	annual	2 to 11	upright	yellow, orange, red, bicolor	early summer until frost	full sun	moderate to high	38, 189
Tagetes tenufolia	signet marigold	annual	2 to 11	upright	yellow, orange, red, bicolor	early summer until frost	full sun	moderate to high	207
Thaumatophyllum xanadu	xanadu philodendron	perennial	10	mounding	white spadix	spring and summer	part shade to shade	moderate	65
Thymus vulgaris	thyme	herbaceous perennial, treated as annual	5 to 9	clumping	white, lavender	spring and early summer	full sun to part sun	moderate	51

BOTANICAL NAME	COMMON NAME(S)	PLANT TYPE	HARDINESS ZONES	GROWTH HABIT	COLORS	BLOOM TIME	SUN	WATER	FEATURED ON PAGE(S)
Tillandsia usneoides	Spanish moss	evergreen	8 to 11	trailing	yellow-green	spring to fall	full sun to part shade	high	115
Tropaeolum majus	nasturtium	annual	2 to 11	mounding, spreading, climbing, trailing	cream, gold, yellow, orange, red, variegated	spring to fall	full sun to part sun	moderate to high	38, 42
Tulbaghia violacea	society garlic	perennial	7 to 10	clumping	lavender	summer and fall	full sun	moderate	68
Tulipa	tulip	perennial bulb	3 to 7	upright	purple, red, orange, yellow, white, pink, bicolor	spring	full sun to part shade	moderate	195
Verbena	verbena	perennial	9 to 11	mounding	orange, reds, pinks, purple, white, bicolor	spring until frost	full sun	moderate	71
Viola cornuta	viola, pansy	perennial, treated as annual	6 to 11	clumping	blues, purples, white, red, yellow, apricot	spring and fall	full sun to part shade	moderate	47, 105, 128, 170, 172
Viola × wittrockiana	pansy	perennial, treated as annual	3 to 8	upright	yellow, red, blue, purple, white, pink, orange, black, multicolored	spring and fall	full sun	moderate to high	105, 128, 132
Zantedeschia	calla lily	perennial bulb	7 to 10	upright, clumping	white, purple, red, orange, yellow, pink	spring until frost	full sun to part sun	moderate to high	60
Zinnia elegans	zinnia	annual	2 to 11	upright	red, yellow, orange, pink, lavender, green, white	summer until frost	full sun	moderate	78

ACKNOWLEDGMENTS

Lindsay, my wife, is my right hand in running The Tender Gardener. Thank you for believing, encouraging, and pushing me through every step of this artistic and creative plant journey. Your optimism and help have been invaluable while I was writing the book and running a business. Thank you for keeping the show going.

A big thank-you to Jennifer Latham for mentioning my name to Kitty Cowles. The first time Kitty and I spoke, I saw a rainbow, and I knew then that this would be a special project. Thank you, Kitty, for turning this dream into a reality by trusting my ideas and visions, for your expert guidance, and for advocating for this book. Thank you for introducing me to your gem of a friend Carrie Brown from Jimtown Store. Carrie, thank you for generously loaning me many containers from your incredible collection. And Kitty, pairing me with Erin Scott was the icing on the cake. Erin, thank you for your warmth, advice, and trust. It was a joy to work with you on the photo shoots. Your expert eye and magic touch behind the camera transformed these arrangements into works of art.

To my mom: thanks for your support, for always listening to me, and for answering all my FaceTime calls to get your keen design advice and opinions, as well as for flying out to help with a photo shoot. And to my sister, Wendy; her partner, Daniel; and my friend Candace: thanks for your excellent energy, assistance, design eyes, and muscle on the photo shoots. My family were the first to share plants with me, and they lit the spark that has led me on this path. We still enjoy trading garden pics and advice.

Bridget Monroe Itkin, you have a gift with words, turning jumbled ideas into clear thoughts. Thank you for your ease and availability. I feel spoiled by your grace and attention. And to the rest of the Artisan team: Lia Ronnen, Zach Greenwald, Laura Cherkas, Paula Brisco, Brooke Beckmann, Suet Chong, Nina Simoneaux, Annie O'Donnell, Nancy Murray, Donna Brown, Erica Huang, Allison McGeehon, Theresa Collier, Amy Michelson, and Brittany Dennison. Thank you for bringing this book to life.

Thank you to Carly Dennet, the owner of Flowerland, for generously loaning me gorgeous containers for the photo shoots, and to Sunny Linvill for all your help around the nursery. Thank you, Troy Stephens, for your helpfulness in finding me plants I was looking for in a pinch. And thank you to the other artists and ceramicists who loaned me pots for the book: Cee Füllemann, Denise Ramos from D. A. R. Studios, and Samantha Carter from Half Light Honey.

Lana Williams is the owner of The Tender Gardener, a plant shop and design company that opened in 2020 in Oakland, California. Her container gardens and landscape designs have been installed at private residences and businesses throughout the Bay Area. She leads local workshops on container gardening, plant care basics, repotting, plant design principles, wreath making, and flower arranging. She has taught plant care classes online and in person at Creativebug and Yelp. When she is not tending to her garden or greenhouse, you can find her in her studio painting and making ceramics. Follow her on Instagram at @The_Tender_Gardener.